THE COMPLETE IDIOT'S GUIDE® TO

Decluttering

DISCARD

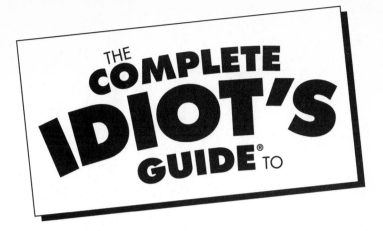

THE
COMPLETE IDIOT'S GUIDE® TO

Decluttering

by Regina Leeds

ALPHA

A member of Penguin Group (USA) Inc.

This book is dedicated with deep love and profound gratitude to my friend and mentor Graham Legerwood.

ALPHA BOOKS

Published by the Penguin Group

Penguin Group (USA) Inc., 375 Hudson Street, New York, New York 10014, U.S.A.

Penguin Group (Canada), 10 Alcorn Avenue, Toronto, Ontario, Canada M4V 3B2 (a division of Pearson Penguin Canada Inc.)

Penguin Books Ltd, 80 Strand, London WC2R 0RL, England

Penguin Ireland, 25 St Stephen's Green, Dublin 2, Ireland (a division of Penguin Books Ltd)

Penguin Group (Australia), 250 Camberwell Road, Camberwell, Victoria 3124, Australia (a division of Pearson Australia Group Pty Ltd)

Penguin Books India Pvt Ltd, 11 Community Centre, Panchsheel Park, New Delhi—110 017, India

Penguin Group (NZ), cnr Airborne and Rosedale Roads, Albany, Auckland 1310, New Zealand (a division of Pearson New Zealand Ltd)

Penguin Books (South Africa) (Pty) Ltd, 24 Sturdee Avenue, Rosebank, Johannesburg 2196, South Africa

Penguin Books Ltd, Registered Offices: 80 Strand, London WC2R 0RL, England

Copyright © 2007 by Regina Leeds

International Standard Book Number: 978-159257-628-9
Library of Congress Catalog Card Number: 2006938598

09 08 07   8 7 6 5 4 3 2 1

Interpretation of the printing code: The rightmost number of the first series of numbers is the year of the book's printing; the rightmost number of the second series of numbers is the number of the book's printing. For example, a printing code of 07-1 shows that the first printing occurred in 2007.

Printed in the United States of America

Note: This publication contains the opinions and ideas of its author. It is intended to provide helpful and informative material on the subject matter covered. It is sold with the understanding that the author and publisher are not engaged in rendering professional services in the book. If the reader requires personal assistance or advice, a competent professional should be consulted.

The author and publisher specifically disclaim any responsibility for any liability, loss, or risk, personal or otherwise, which is incurred as a consequence, directly or indirectly, of the use and application of any of the contents of this book.

Most Alpha books are available at special quantity discounts for bulk purchases for sales promotions, premiums, fund-raising, or educational use. Special books, or book excerpts, can also be created to fit specific needs.

For details, write: Special Markets, Alpha Books, 375 Hudson Street, New York, NY 10014.

Publisher: *Marie Butler-Knight*
Editorial Director: *Mike Sanders*
Managing Editor: *Billy Fields*
Acquisitions Editor: *Paul Dinas*
Senior Development Editor: *Phil Kitchel*
Production Editor: *Kayla Dugger*
Copy Editor: *Krista Hansing Editorial Services, Inc.*

Cover Designer: *Bill Thomas*
Book Designer: *Trina Wurst*
Indexer: *Brad Herriman*
Layout: *Brian Massey*
Proofreader: *John Etchison*

Contents at a Glance

Contents

Appendixes

Introduction

Myriad reasons exist for why people are not organized. The most common is, quite simply, no one ever taught you! Organizing is at its heart a skill that anyone can learn. Moving out from that center, we find a cornucopia of reasons why it isn't part of your life: perhaps your mother was a neat freak and chaos is how you have chosen to rebel. It doesn't matter that Mom is long dead and you have reached retirement age.

Tracing your personal history, you might discover that you were always organized and then the birth of your last baby pushed you over the edge. Juggling a home, a career, a spouse, and motherhood have seemed insurmountable. You might also be caught in the vise of that age-old double-sided terror, fear of success and fear of failure. Getting it all together seems like too much responsibility, no matter which way you cut it.

Unwanted or sudden change can also knock you off the organized path right into the clutches of depression. Perhaps someone close to you died or you had to move to a new city to accommodate your spouse's career. The launch pad into depression is varied. You can be there for a long time before you realize you aren't getting out of bed, much less making it.

While the scope of this book is narrow and we are not at liberty to delve into your past and find out why you are living in chaos, we can identify one common denominator. Unorganized people avoid, delay, or simply do not make decisions. That's how clutter is created. Item by item enters the environment, and no one knows what to do with it. To use this book effectively, you need to make just one decision: decide to use it as your guide to an organized life. Step by step through all the rooms of your home or office, we're going to make a journey out of chaos into order.

Extras

Along the way, you'll find tips and tidbits that will help you. Here's what you'll find in each box:

Perilous Pitfalls

We all learn from our mistakes, right? These guidelines will enable you to bypass the typical learning curve we face with any organizational challenge or project. You'll skate right to the high-productivity area!

Timely Tidbits

Everyone wants to know the tips and tricks professional organizers use to achieve success. I've shared the secrets of my 18 years of organizing experience in order to help you easily conquer your clutter!

Acknowledgments

I had always envied writers. They work at home. They make their own hours. I thought it was a pretty cushy way to make a living. And then I wrote my first book. Writing a book is like being consumed in a volatile relationship. The book is all you can think about. Inspiration strikes at all hours of the day or night. Friends and family take you away from your focus. At the end of the workday, you feel like a rag doll tossed into the corner of a playroom by a careless child. As they say in my old neighborhood in Brooklyn: "Who knew?"

They're right, you know. It takes a village. This time out, my village was populated by three irreplaceable and irrepressible angels. Marilyn Allen is my literary agent and my friend. She is a woman of grace and tenderness whose belief in me has been appreciated since the day we met. Thank you, Marilyn.

If Marilyn opened the door to the world of "The Idiot's Guides," it was acquisitions editor Paul Dinas who showed me around. Every time (and there were many) that I wanted to throw in the towel, Paul not only guided me, he made me laugh. You gotta love a guy who takes you from frustration to laughter in seconds. Thank you, Paul, for your patience, your guidance, and your humor.

The last person in my tiny village is the one who is always in my corner, my best friend, Susie Ribnik. I was able to master the Idiot's writing formula. I couldn't begin to grasp the setup format. That kind of detail takes the patience of a saint and computer knowledge I don't have. Susie read the instruction manual and thought it was well written and easy to follow. I read it and was overwhelmed, sleepy, and confused. I thank God for you, Susie.

I wish to thank the wonderful folks at The Container Store. Every step of the way, as they have with all of my projects, The Container Store supported me in any way they could. The store is an organizer's dream; the PR department is a writer's best friend.

Finally, I want to thank all of my clients. They have opened their homes and their lives to me. It is they who have taught me what I put into this book. They have all been my teachers, and many have become dear friends. My profound thanks extend to all of them for all time.

Trademarks

All terms mentioned in this book that are known to be or are suspected of being trademarks or service marks have been appropriately capitalized. Alpha Books and Penguin Group (USA) Inc. cannot attest to the accuracy of this information. Use of a term in this book should not be regarded as affecting the validity of any trademark or service mark.

What Is a Cluttered Home?

In This Chapter

- ◆ Deciding if you have one
- ◆ Winning the war against clutter
- ◆ Creating systems to keep the order
- ◆ Getting started if you're totally overwhelmed

Most of us know a cluttered home on sight. It's difficult to find a place to sit. Every surface seems to hold a stack of papers, magazines, or newspapers. Trying to find something is like searching for the proverbial needle in a haystack. Daily dramas like the old "Where are my keys?" routine keep the home in turmoil. Time is wasted and money flies out the door as you keep buying things you already have. We get so used to the chaos and drama, it feels as if there is no way out.

Well, you know what they say: we've got good news and we've got bad news. The bad news is that you're living in an environment that makes life far more difficult than it needs to be.

The good news is that you created it and you can put something new in its place.

The Warning Signs

Here's a quick checklist designed to help you recognize the common warning signs of a cluttered environment. How many of these statements reflect how you feel about your home?

- Items in my dresser drawers are usually too wrinkled to wear.

- Wow! I didn't realize how prosperous I was. Isn't that what stuff indicates?

- No matter which way my weight goes, I've got a wardrobe in my closet to fit my body!

- I'm thinking of opening a beauty supply shop with all the products I have in my bathroom. Too bad most of the lotions and potions have expired.

- There's so much junk mail piled up, I haven't seen my kitchen counter or dining room table in years! That's okay—we love take-out.

- I wonder what it would be like to put the car in the garage.

- I don't wash the dishes until all the clean ones are piled high in the sink. Why waste the time and energy washing a few dishes at a time?

- I've never understood the importance of making my bed. Won't it just get rumpled again tonight?

- My kids' toys are everywhere! I can't seem to get the kids to pick up after themselves.

Timely Tidbits

Ever wonder where clutter comes from? Every time you say, "I have no idea where this goes—I'll just toss it here," you add to the chaos in your home. Clutter is the physical result of unmade decisions.

Please take a minute now to write down your personal warning signs.

Record all the little everyday dramas that make you feel exhausted, desperate, and longing for a home that nurtures and supports you in body, mind, and soul.

Keep this list handy; we're going to refer to it often. A notebook or journal is the ideal way to record your notes and thoughts. I'll have a few more assignments for you scattered throughout this book. In fact, I am going to refer to this journal as your *Declutter Notebook.*

How Do You Eat an Elephant?

Everybody knows the punch line to that one: one bite at a time. Guess what? That's exactly how you are going to get organized.

Considering any task in its entirety is overwhelming. You may be feeling tired already, thinking, "I can't get organized, my situation is too far gone." On the other hand, you may be tempted to make a mad dash around the house, picking things up and stuffing them randomly into drawers and closets.

Please don't. Nor do I want you to have projects going in every room of the house. Avoid being overwhelmed and embrace feeling in control and confident by breaking down every project into parts. Later in this book, we'll go through every room in the home, and I'll give you all the step-by-step instruction your heart desires.

Work That System

Believe it or not, all the chaos and drama in your life is part of a carefully worked out, albeit unconscious, system that you have adhered to with the tenacity of a religious zealot. You may say that you abhor the "Where are my keys?" drama, but you don't change the behavior, do you? On some level, this and all the little dramas of your life have become the norm. It's part of the system you have in place.

In this chapter, we lay the foundation for a new system in your home and your life. I've given you an arsenal of tips and tricks that will keep you organized. You'll be able to pick and choose which ones suit you. Your new system will be unique to you. You will work it with the same tenacity that you now work the unconscious system that makes you miserable.

Hidden Treasure

Every so often, I am invited into a home that appears perfect to the eye. I wonder why this client has called me. In a few minutes, though, I get permission to peer into what I call the secret areas of the home, and there, behind closet doors and stuffed into drawers, are volcanic eruptions of stuff.

Is this how you got "organized" in the past? Perhaps it was a major holiday, company was coming, or you were just fed up. You scooped things up in your arms and started stuffing. Maybe you even took the opportunity to dust and vacuum and declare that you had gotten organized. Guess what? You only tidied up.

Getting organized means you've put a system in place. In an organized home, every drawer and closet works to support the lives of those in the home. My mother was a super-organized person, but she never bothered to organize her closets and drawers. Mom said no one saw them, so they didn't matter. Guess what? We saw them, so it absolutely did matter. Our environments have a profound influence on our mental clarity and physical health. Even if you tightly shut the doors and drawers, the chaos will affect you.

Pockets of Unrest

Let's play a game, shall we? I want you to leave your home. If you can, take a minute and walk around the block or go for coffee. When you return, pretend you've never been here before. What does looking around tell you about the person or family that lives here? Are they tidy? Is every room in an uproar? Or do you notice specific problem areas?

You may learn that the clutter is limited to closets and drawers. Or perhaps they have the most beautifully set up closets you have ever seen—and a kitchen with not a single inch of free counter space. Pretending this isn't your stuff will help you distance your emotions and engage your brain in the organizing process. I also hope that maybe you'll come away feeling that this isn't as bad as you imagined.

It's one thing to make mental notes; it's another to write your findings down on paper. Therefore, please list all the rooms in your home on a sheet of paper, preferably in the notebook you chose for this journey. Next to each room, list every project you think needs to be tended to in each area. Be concise.

Remember when I said anything is overwhelming in its entirety? When you see your list on paper, it will be easier to begin your organizing. Free-floating, fear-based ideas like "I am never going to get organized!" or "There's so much to do here; it's hopeless!" will only feed that over-whelmed feeling. Now you can look at a concrete list of projects and put them in order of importance.

Tipping the Scales in Your Favor

Some of you have simply never been taught the skill of getting organized. You will absorb the step-by-step instruction I've provided here and be on your way to an organized life in no time. For those for whom chaos is an emotional as well as instructional journey, take heart. At every juncture, I give you tools to calm your fears.

If you are looking at your newly prioritized list and feel overwhelmed instead of in control, here's what to do. Put your list aside. Think up some things you could do every single day that would result in an improved environment. These need to be simple, repeatable actions. Jot them down in your journal. Here are my favorite choices:

◆ Make the bed every morning when you get up.

◆ Never leave dirty dishes in the sink.

◆ Put clean dishes away immediately.

◆ Take the garbage out every day, preferably at the same time.

◆ And (my personal favorite) put your keys in the same place every time you enter the home.

Psychologists say it takes 21 *consecutive* days of repeating an action before it becomes a habit. Therefore, pick one, two, or three (no more, to start) things you would like to turn into habits. Begin today. Put a mark in your day planner or on your calendar in red ink every time you perform this action.

In three short weeks, you will have done more than establish new habits; you will have shifted the energy in your home. Your self-esteem will grow as you begin to accomplish small things. All those with whom you share your environment will be affected. In families in which good relationships have been formed, these subtle shifts invite everyone to get involved. Encourage others to learn how to get organized through your good example, not your tirades and pleas.

The Least You Need to Know

◆ Getting organized is a teachable skill that anyone can master.

◆ The old saying "There is a place for everything and everything belongs in its place" is at the heart of an organized home.

◆ Creating new, simple habits shifts the environment and sets you on the road to getting and staying organized.

◆ Anything is overwhelming in its entirety; we gain control over any project when we break it down into simple steps.

Chapter 2

How Do We Take the First Decluttering Step?

In This Chapter

- ◆ Assess the clutter issues in your home
- ◆ Set realistic goals
- ◆ Establish a timetable for completion
- ◆ Learn the formula that will conquer clutter
- ◆ Decide if you need help and what is available

How do you take the first step? You decide to change. There it is. Just as clutter is the collected debris of unmade decisions, order is the result of a series of decisions that you make and stick to. It's like Nike's famous ad says: "Just do it!"

That said, decluttering is a big job, so let's set ourselves up to win the War Against Stuff.

Take Stock

If I came to your home to help you declutter, I would ask where you wanted to begin. People always have very definite ideas about the worst clutter culprits in the home. Perhaps you hate how mail and school papers gather on your kitchen counter. Or maybe you're tired of never being able to walk into your closet, much less find anything. I like to see the problem, and then I always ask if I can tour the rest of the home.

See Yourself in This Story?

One day a mother told me we needed to begin in her child's room. Now, it's not uncommon for teenagers to rebel by using the state of their rooms to make Mom and Dad climb the walls, but it was unusual for a parent to want to begin the decluttering of the home in her child's room. I was curious to see if the rest of the home was indeed clutter-free and perfectly organized. As you might imagine, it wasn't.

Very often emotional issues swirl around your home along with the clutter. This mom didn't want to face the clutter in *her* bedroom, so she decided to try working with me on neutral territory: her child's room. We judge ourselves harshly when the environment falls apart. Just remember, it's probably a clutter zone because something happened to throw you off your game or no one ever taught you how to be organized. In either case, it's a fixable issue.

> **Timely Tidbits**
> We learn how to clutter our environments. It takes some time and effort to learn how to declutter them and keep them debris-free.

What's the Real Deal?

Please grab your *Declutter Notebook* and let's take a tour of your home or apartment. Before we begin, make a list of all the rooms in the home. Even if you live in a studio apartment, you have areas designated for specific activities, which function as your "rooms." I grew up in New York City and have experienced living in everything from an entire brownstone to a matchbox-size studio. We humans manage to create zones of activity regardless of the size of the space.

Devote a separate piece of paper to each room or area. As you enter the room, shut off your emotions and your judgment. Turn on your analytical left brain. All you need to do is make a list of the projects you see that will bring this room to order. Let me give you an example.

Most family rooms have a virtual explosion of stuff. Here is a common list of projects for a typical family room. See if you can relate. You can create a parallel shopping list, if you like, of the items you need, such as a new CD tower.

- Organize toys.

- Put all electronic entertainment components in order: VHS tapes, DVDs, CDs, and so on.

- Create a hobby zone for _____ (photo albums, scrapbooking, etc.).

- Reduce the physical clutter by eliminating some items on the walls or a few pieces of furniture.

When you have your list, put your rooms in order of priority. For me, the typical home space works best if organized in this order:

1. Master bedroom

2. Master bath

3. Kitchen

4. Home office or work area

5. Family room

6. Kids' rooms

7. Guest rooms (if any)

8. Ancillary areas: garage, basement, attic, laundry, etc.

This order enables you to begin your day in peace and calm. Not only will you be more relaxed as you tackle the rest of the home, but you also will be teaching your children by your good example. Saying to your child, "I want you to declutter your room and get organized," isn't as powerful as living the example.

The World of Realistic Goals

Clutter doesn't happen overnight; it grows over time into a serious problem that compels you to purchase a book like this. Therefore, it will take some time to reverse the situation. I tell my clients that even if time and money are no object, I don't like to do too many projects in a short span of time. It's best to do one room a week, if possible. Enjoy the order and see if the organized area makes you feel different than the chaotic rooms do. I promise you, it will. This will give you encouragement and motivation to continue.

Do you have a goal in mind for your home? Let's say you buy this book in August, and you'd like to have your extended family over for Thanksgiving. You have a nice block of time to schedule your projects and surprise your relatives.

Look into your future and find a target date, such as Thanksgiving. Mark your calendar in red with something like "Clutter-Free Day." Now count your projects and see how many weeks you have. Do the math and see how much time you have for each project. Don't rush or push yourself unrealistically. If you're walking to a destination, it's one step at a time, isn't it? Same principle applies here: one step, one project at a time to a decluttered and organized home.

Are you starting to feel less overwhelmed and in control? That's the goal. Piece-by-piece decluttering is really like putting together a big three-dimensional jigsaw puzzle. This whole process has elements of fun and the opportunity to express your creativity. Look for those experiences along the way.

Set a Schedule

Okay, you have a list of projects and you have figured out how much overall time you have for each. The next step is to be realistic about your life. For example, perhaps you are a stay-at-home mom and you want to organize your kitchen. This is usually a fairly large room with a lot of stuff. I would allow one day to declutter and another for organizing. You really need a block of five uninterrupted hours for your projects so you can really make some progress. Much the same way, if you work full-time, you will probably have to sacrifice a few weekends.

When Time Is Tight

If setting aside at least five hours makes you balk, ask yourself whether you are really ready to declutter right now or whether you are giving it lip service. Perhaps family and friends are pressuring you. If you know in your heart that you aren't ready, put it off until you are. Victor Hugo said, "There is nothing as powerful as an idea whose time has come." He didn't have decluttering in mind, but I think the wisdom applies.

Perilous Pitfalls

Whether you use a calendar, your computer, or a daily planner, be sure to write down your goals and set specific dates for completing your projects. Otherwise, the changes you hope to make will stay in the realm of wishful thinking.

The Exception to the Rule

Some professional organizers suggest working in 15-minute increments. I have to say that this advice makes me cringe. This might work for a select few—for example, those who are clinically depressed, those who are physically handicapped in some way, or moms with infants and/or toddlers in the home. Young children live in the "now," and reality for them *never* includes getting organized.

There are ways around the time crunch, which we deal with a few paragraphs later. For now, be realistic and set aside some serious time by making an official appointment with yourself.

Timely Tidbits

We reach our goals in life by respecting and honoring the steps we have to take to achieve them. No cluttered home was created in an hour. Nor will it spring to order in minutes. You need to really want to make the clutter go away. Success requires a serious commitment on your part, especially when it comes to your time.

Gather Your Supplies

As we work our way through each chapter, I suggest items that will help you get the clutter out and the order in. Chief among these are sturdy garbage bags. I prefer the lawn and garden variety; they hold more and are less likely to tear.

I will also introduce you to some of my favorite products from The Container Store. Sometimes an area is in chaos, and introducing a few organizing tools can make it snap to order. If you don't live near The Container Store but you have access to the web, be sure to check out their website, www.thecontainerstore.com. You can go to specific areas at the site and get product ideas tailored for the items we keep in the kitchen, bathroom, garage, and so on. Many more product ideas are included than I could possibly cover here. You'll also have access to free design help for some home projects.

Choosing the right organizing products is one of the fun elements of decluttering, and it doesn't have to cost an arm and a leg. In fact, many products can serve one purpose now and another in a few months or years. You might purchase some large containers on wheels to store your child's toys and in a few years be using them to store holiday ornaments. A good-quality product will stand the test of time.

Don't Forget Your Body

The day before I meet clients for the first time, I tell them I have some advice for them. I know I sound like a mother, but the decluttering/ organizing process is physically, mentally, and emotionally draining. To meet the demands of your projects, you need to do the following:

◆ Get a good night's sleep.

◆ Work at the time of day when you are at your peak. We are usually divided into morning people and night people. You know which you prefer.

◆ Have a nourishing meal before you start. I'm talking about brain food, not a candy bar.

◆ Speaking of the latter, you'll want lots of water and healthful snacks at hand. When your blood sugar drops, a candy bar will give you a quick lift; a piece of cheese or some fresh fruit will sustain you for hours.

♦ Don't forget to make your environment as inviting as possible. I relish working in silence. Most of my clients like music in the background. What do you like?

♦ Finally, we're all kids at heart: plan a reward. Maybe a bubble bath or a night at the movies will float your boat. Only you can decide what it will be. The bigger the challenge of the area you are tackling, the more important it is to have something to look forward to. Hey, what about that candy bar?

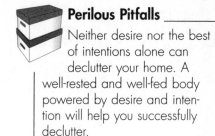

Perilous Pitfalls

Neither desire nor the best of intentions alone can declutter your home. A well-rested and well-fed body powered by desire and intention will help you successfully declutter.

The Magic Formula

I coined this phrase almost 20 years ago when I started my business. I noticed that all organizing projects had similarities. I organized them in the same order—only the "stuff" changed. Whether it's the paper in your office, the clothing in your closet, or the toys and magazines in the family room, the process is the same:

1. **Eliminate** what you don't need.

2. **Categorize** what you are keeping.

3. **Organize** those categories.

Eliminate

Eliminate everything that no longer belongs in the space. This can mean tossing items that are now trash (my clients will swear this is my favorite activity), donating things to a charity, returning items you borrowed from others, taking things to the room in which they really belong, or archiving items you have to keep but that you don't need in your everyday environment. Income tax returns are a great example of the latter.

Categorize

The great feature about the Magic Formula is that the second step comes organically out of the first. As you work item by item making your decisions, some things will, of course, stay. You create categories as you go along.

The closet is an easy example. Your categories may be tops, slacks, suits, shoes, and ties. Think about your favorite store. All its goods are in categories or departments, and everything in those areas is organized. Ever notice the chaos of a sale rack? We're going from sale rack to upscale boutique all over your home.

Organize

When you have your categories, you need to figure out the best way to organize them. Without a system, the clutter will return faster than you can read the title of this book! I like all of my finished decluttering projects to be beautiful to look at, completely functional, and able to absorb more.

Timely Tidbits

The three surefire steps to decluttering success are to eliminate, categorize, and organize!

I call this three-step formula *magical* because you can apply it to any challenge you have. It will help you work on projects at work. The kids can apply it to homework assignments. Planning a party? Going on a trip? The Magic Formula is your key to success.

Go It Alone, or It Takes a Village?

If clutter is such an issue for you that you need help, just be sure you ask the right person. You want someone who is organized and who lives a clutter-free life. We all have those friends and relatives! Perhaps you just want the company and someone's suggestions as you do the physical work. Your goal is to learn from this person. Avoid people who will bully you or dispense shame every time they open their mouths.

A Family Affair: Chores for Everyone

When you are part of a family unit, every person needs to pitch in and contribute time and talents. Chores for children build self-esteem and also teach them how to run a home. After all, you don't want your children to go off to college or get married without a clue of how to do laundry or cook a meal. Chores are a privilege, not a punishment.

Professional Organizer to the Rescue

I have been organizing clients for close to 20 years. The men and women who call me are highly intelligent and very successful. They aren't idiots! Getting organized is a skill that many of us never learned. If you weren't taught as a child, how would you know how to declutter an environment, much less teach your own children?

If you don't have any organized family members or friends, or if you would be embarrassed to ask them for help even if you did, consider hiring a professional organizer. Many of us have specialties. Some do only homes, some offices; others, like me, do it all.

One day one of my clients looked at me in the middle of a big project and said, "Now I know who you are. You're the nonjudgmental, non-shaming mother we all wish we'd had." I have to say the compliment made me blush and laugh at the same time. A good professional organizer is really your teacher and guide.

The Least You Need to Know

- A plan is key to your success.
- Any clutter challenge will yield to order if you remember to eliminate, categorize, and organize.
- Asking a family member, trusted friend, or professional organizer to help you declutter will make the process faster.
- Everyone in the home needs to contribute to the order by being responsible for chores.

Chapter 3

Maintaining the Organized Home

In This Chapter

- ◆ Learn how to maintain the order you create
- ◆ Watch your positive habits multiply
- ◆ Discover clever ways to make donations and recycle
- ◆ Figure out how to enlist your family
- ◆ Store it or toss it: ways to decide

I had a professor in college who was very wise and had a great deal of influence over me. One day she told the class that some people are naturally gifted in some areas. Although this appears to be a blessing, it might actually be a curse. When it all comes easy, you can forget a basic tenet of life: to achieve, you have to *do something*.

And so it is with the clutter-free house: you have to do something to get it that way and keep doing it to keep it that way. The payoff is enormous: you get to live in a home that is a peaceful, calm oasis from a crazy world; you save time you used to waste searching for things; you save money because you know exactly what you have and what you need; your self-esteem is higher from a job well done; and, last but not least, you teach your children a skill that will serve them in every aspect of their lives. As Martha Stewart likes to say, "It's a good thing."

A Good System Is Key

People repeatedly write to me or ask me in my class why they constantly have to get reorganized. They tell me they spent time, got the place looking great—and two weeks later, poof! All the clutter was back. I tell them they tidied up, but they didn't get organized. Tidying up will get you decluttered for about two weeks. It's a good strategy if all you care about is looking good for company or around the holidays. The latter (getting organized) means a *system* is in place. It's a system that you create and tweak as the demands of the moment and time dictate. Most of all, it's a system that you honor.

Remember to Multiply the *Power of Three*

In Chapter 1, I suggested that you jump-start the decluttering process by creating three positive new habits. When you establish, for example, that taking out the trash is something that you do rain or shine each night right after dinner, you may begin to think about creating another new habit … or two … or three ….

Take out your *Declutter Notebook* and jot down some things you think would make life easier in your home if only you did these things consistently. The big one, of course, is putting keys in the same place every time you enter the home. For you, perhaps keeping track of your reading glasses, cellphone, or TV remote is more of an issue. Everything that bothers you has a cure. See if you can't work those cures into your daily life one at a time.

> **Perilous Pitfalls**
>
> Repeating an action for 21 days will make it a habit. However, it must be 21 *consecutive* days. If you miss a day, you need to start fresh. Blame the psychologists who discovered the pattern.

Calling in the Troops

I don't like to see anyone make a big deal out of decluttering as a way to get the family involved. Grand announcements at the dinner table about how "this family is going to change" can set you up for failure. Throughout this book, you will hear me say that I believe in the power of teaching by example. Don't *order* your family to join your war on clutter—entice them.

The Power of Chores

The people you share your life with have co-responsibility with you to make the home run smoothly and be clutter-free. If you have difficulty getting your children to do chores, perhaps you need to enforce consequences. Do they treasure computer time? Do they enjoy chatting with friends on the phone? Is there an open-door policy for friends on the weekend? Whatever floats their boat goes out the window when the chores aren't done. By the same token, you could reward them with points for consistent service.

Bringing in Outside Help

Sometimes the help you need lies outside the home. I am thinking about cleaning assistance. I'm not talking about anything as grand as live-in help—just calling a service if your clutter has prevented you from cleaning your home for a while. After you declutter, let the service give your home a good once-over.

Perhaps you could stay on top of things more easily if you had someone come in once or twice a month, or once a quarter. Only you know what you need and what you can afford. The important thing is to understand that it isn't failure to ask for help; it's the sign of victory. With regular chores and occasional outside assistance, clutter will be permanently banished from your home. It's teamwork in action!

Storing Stuff

It's hard to imagine a home or apartment where nothing needs to be stored. I suppose if you're a member of a strict religious order, you might be a possession-free person. The rest of us will always need to store some stuff.

If you have a large home, don't kid yourself into thinking that you can save everything because, after all, "we have the space." You are avoiding decision making and are probably helping a close family member do the same. What happens when it comes time to downsize and live in a smaller place? You'll be inundated with the unmade decisions of a lifetime in the form of furniture, memorabilia, toys, photos, and all manner of things.

I presume you're inspired to read this book and get to work removing all the clutter from your environment. On the off chance you just might have a few items to store away, what do you do? I am so glad you asked!

Home Storage

Let's face it: the homeowner has an easier time. The bigger the home, the more storage space exists. When I was growing up on the East Coast, it seemed like everyone had lots of closets, a finished basement or an attic, and maybe even a garage—a bonanza of space, by anyone's standards. Yet take heart if you live in an apartment. Even the tiniest studio dweller can discover storage areas, if you know where to look.

We'll talk about things like adding shelves to closets. You'll learn the secret ways to gain more space in any closet, such as removing the extra wire hangers and plastic bags from the cleaners. The results are amazing. Learn the wonders of space bags. Don't neglect high shelves if you are short: use a step stool.

Try using furniture that serves a double purpose. You can sit on that trunk at the foot of your bed as it quietly stores your extra winter blankets. The beautiful rattan or leather containers by your living room chair can hold the lamp that allows you to read each evening. When you need to pay bills, the containers might house your active files. Right now you can't see the trees because the forest of clutter is so thick. When you clear the debris, you will see clearly what's available to you.

Public Storage

Sometimes you don't have a choice, but public storage is never my first choice for a client. It will cost you money to keep this stuff, so it had better be valuable or a temporary situation.

Do your homework before you embrace this choice. Be sure you visit the site before you arrive with your belongings. Here are some things to consider before selecting the off-site storage facility:

- Is the facility well maintained?
- Is it well lit?
- Are the hours of operation convenient?
- Is it close to your home, in case you have to make a quick run to either retrieve or leave an item?
- Do the walls separating your unit from your neighbors' go all the way up to the ceiling?
- Will your homeowner's policy cover you in the event of loss, or do you need to purchase the insurance being offered?

I have seen clients rent public storage space to house the strangest items. One client got a space for the empty boxes his computer and entertainment equipment had come in. Yes, he had that many boxes. He wanted to be sure he had the original boxes in the event of a move. Guess what? Movers have boxes and packing made for this purpose. The most expensive mover in town would have been cheaper than the space he rented. Be sure you really need the items you're storing. Whatever their value, it's going to cost you.

It's Outta Here

Many years ago, I had a client who was hesitant to throw anything away. He was afraid he would make a mistake. I tell my clients that unless they carelessly toss items we know we all need (think birth certificates, current passports, tax returns, etc.), you can't make a mistake. There are rules for legal papers. For example, ask your tax advisor how long you need to keep tax records. Talk to your attorney or real estate agent about real estate transaction papers. Seek out the professional who counsels you in any given area if you are confused. With a phone call or two, you won't make a mistake! There's common sense for everything else.

Let's return to my client. The first piece of paper we looked at was a letter he no longer needed. I suggested that he toss it. He balked. And then he did it … and kept doing it for several hours. We had several huge bags of trash when we were done. He was as giddy and delighted as a child. Tossing what you no longer need is freeing. Join my client: be brave and take that first step.

Think Beyond the Blue Bin

The blue bin is, of course, your recycling can. However, there are many ways to recycle. Be creative! Here are four things I can think of that classify as creative recycling. What can you add?

1. Take stacks of magazines to senior homes or hospitals.

2. Do you have extra plain or colored paper that you won't be using? Perhaps you just moved and you have a roll of plain packing paper from the movers? Take this to your local grammar school for the kids in kindergarten or the after-school program to draw on.

3. Don't like to donate clothes to a national charity because you prefer to know where your things are going? Call your local houses of worship and get connected to a poor family. Watch your things find new life in another home.

4. Are you a typical mom who is attached to your baby's special outfits? Baby, of course, is soon going to college, but that's another story. Call your local children's hospital or charity that helps sick or terminal kids. I'll bet those children (and their parents) would have their spirits lifted by a beautiful new outfit.

Dumpster Diving

Sometimes my clients have a lifetime's worth of stuff, and getting the trash out will take a Herculean task. Check your local Yellow Pages and find a dumpster rental. They come in all sizes. You fill it up and, when you're ready, the company returns and hauls it all away.

By the way, refrain from the other kind of dumpster diving. You know, you're minding your business taking a Sunday drive. Suddenly you see an old chair cast out on the street. You take it home, thinking, "One day I might need this." Let's bring home only what you need today. There are a lot of chairs out there in the world. When you're ready, one will appear.

Support Your Local Charity

Many charities will accept your donation because they have thrift stores where they sell the items. Take a good look at what you have and see if you can benefit any such organizations. For example, the local high school might want your old computers and printers. So might the local trade school. If you are creative with your donations, you can get excited about this declutter mission we're about to embark on instead of viewing it as a punishment or homework assignment. It will do you good. It can also benefit others.

Let's Not Forget eBay or Craig's List

If you wish you could afford a cleaning person for a day or the guidance of a professional organizer, or perhaps you'd like to plan a big reward for doing this work, why not sell some of your things on eBay? The best news is that many people now do this for a living. You can probably find someone by putting out the word with family and friends.

Or you can go to www.i-soldit.com; they have stores across the country that sell items for people on eBay. Yes, everyone does work by commission. But whatever you get will be more than you would have had if the items had just stayed with you and collected dust.

If the commission issue is insurmountable for you, go to Craig's List online. You can take a digital picture of your treasure and have it up in seconds. There's no fee. Craig survives on advertising. I am not a very computer-savvy person, and I was able to open an account in seconds. Have a problem? Find a teenager. They all know how to work the Internet.

Keeper of the Flame—the Family Archivist

In every family, one person is the family archivist. This person keeps all the kids' things after they go off to college. In fact, those kids now have kids, but their houses are smaller, so they want you to hold on to their stuff. Or perhaps you are one of several children, and when your parents died, you took everyone's inherited family heirlooms to keep until they have room for them. You've been waiting more than 20 years to send their things to them, but why rush?

Remember when I said that clutter is the result of unmade decisions? This kind of debris is the result of several people in your life refusing to make their own decisions. Free yourself. Ask them to rent a U-Haul. If they balk, tell them you're renting one and ask whether they want you to open a storage account for them or deliver their stuff to their homes. If they live far away, assure them that you will make the charity donation in their name. You need your space back for yourself. That's *your* decision.

Life Happens

No matter how carefully you put your new system in place and no matter how devoted you are to it, life will toss you a curveball from time to time. Your spouse might get the flu and give it to all the kids. Just as they get well, you might be knocked flat on your back. Or perhaps there is a death in the family and you have to travel for a few days to get to the funeral. You return home and feel too depressed to deal with the mail. A few weeks then go by, and suddenly you wonder where all this clutter came from.

Take heart. Whatever the scenario, the bottom line is that life happens. The beauty of a system is that it's waiting for you to reinstate it. You don't have to reinvent the wheel; you just have to restore order. That's a different ballgame from decluttering a house that is run without rhyme or reason. Expect life to happen. The system will allow you to return to normal.

The Home Inventory

When the clutter is gone, you'll find yourself living with my mother's favorite slogan: "There's a place for everything, and everything belongs in its place. The next time you need it, you'll know exactly where to find it." Well, why not document it so that if it ever vanishes—say, in a fire, flood, earthquake, or terrorist attack—you'll have something to present to insurance?

In this day and age, you can record items using a video recorder or digital camera. If you have very valuable items, such as furs, jewelry, or artwork, get a professional appraisal. All this documentation can be kept in a safety deposit box or a fireproof container in your home. It takes a few hours to create your inventory, but it can save weeks of work.

The Least You Need to Know

- Emergencies may interrupt the order in your home from time to time, but you can restore the order if you have a system in place.

- With a little creativity and research, donating things that you no longer need can be a rewarding journey.

- A home inventory will save you time and money if you experience a home disaster and need to deal with your insurance company.

4

Kitchen: Is Yours the Hub of Your Home?

In This Chapter

- Clear the space of your broken, expired, or no-longer-used items
- Pinpoint exactly what does and does not work in this room
- Create work zones for prep, cooking, baking, and cleanup
- Explore products that can maximize your use of the space

Do you ever wonder why people seem to gather in the kitchen? Have you ever been to a party where the majority of the people were anywhere else? No matter how crowded, no matter how small, there we all are. Perhaps we're unconsciously emulating our ancestors who gathered around the campfire. Or maybe we just like food!

Let's take a cold, hard look at what's going on in your kitchen. As with all the rooms in your home, I hope you find that things are not as bad as you presumed. And if they are, just follow my directions and you'll be the Martha Stewart of your neighborhood in no time.

Assessment: What's Here and What Tools Do I Need?

What is your chief complaint about your kitchen? Take a minute to look around and ask yourself these questions. They will help you zone in on the specific issues you face.

- Have my counters become a dumping ground for mail, school papers, and miscellaneous items in search of a home?

- If I open a drawer, is there a haphazard mixture of kitchen tools? In other words, does the meat grinder live next to the rolling pin?

- Am I using pots and pans from the Stone Age?

- Are my mixing bowls and other ceramic or glass tools chipped and cracked?

- Is there any rhyme or reason to the way the cupboards are organized?

- Do family members put items back in the designated spot, or is it a free-for-all?

- Are my cupboards so deep that items vanish in the deepest recesses? Or are they so narrow that I can't store anything bigger than a small container of spice?

For the Sake of Balance

What works for you? Do you like having your sink by a window so you can look out when you wash the dishes? Do you have a large pantry that you keep stocked with the basics? Did you get a set of new pots and pans for your birthday?

Acknowledge everything that works and take a minute or two to record your thoughts in your *Declutter Notebook*.

Tools of the Trade

As in every room, you'll need heavy-duty lawn bags or empty boxes to haul away what no longer serves you. Perhaps a combination would be best. If you prefer boxes, visit your local liquor store or supermarket and ask for a few. I am sure they will be happy to comply.

I'll be introducing you to some great products from The Container Store to help make your kitchen sing as we go through this chapter. Let's set the kitchen-decluttering machine in motion!

The Quick Fix

You're going to need to be in ruthless mode right now. It's time to make decisions. Make them quickly, and trust that they are in the best interests of this room and how you and your family use it. This is not the time to cry over the potato peeler that your late Auntie Jessie left you (if she were alive, she'd have a new one). It's down-and-dirty time. In about one hour, you are going to change the energy in your kitchen and be on your way to creating a room that you not only enjoy, but also love to share with family and friends.

By the way, you don't need to do anything with the things you know you want to keep—yet. This first phase is about decluttering the space by removing the items that no longer serve you. Whether you're a gourmet cook or someone who barely boils water, this room is going to be a lean, mean food-support machine!

> **Timely Tidbits**
>
> Tossing items is not wasteful if you no longer use them, have never used them, can't identify them, or see that they are broken or expired. What's wasteful is crowding your life and personal environment with stuff and robbing yourself of valuable space, time, and energy.

Does Anybody Remember What This Is?

Let's start with food. Go to your pantry or food cupboard and toss any expired cans, bags, or boxes. If you have lots of staples like flour, how are they stored? I once had an invasion of pantry moths. You want to keep food items like flour, sugar, pasta, and nuts in airtight containers. Do you need some? Add that to your shopping list.

Open your refrigerator and freezer and toss any old food items. Remember, freezing doesn't put food into suspended animation forever. It's good for about four to six months. Can't identify it? It's outta here.

Are Your Drawers Stuck?

After you toss the old food, move on to the drawers. Toss any old, rusted, broken, can't-identify, or no-longer-used items.

In addition to cooking tools, everyone has a "junk drawer." You know the one. You've got tacks, nails, tape, a hammer, phone numbers, expired coupons, scrap paper, pens, gum, and surely one batch of keys you can't identify. Let's clean this one out as well. It's okay to have a "miscellaneous" drawer, but the real junk has to go.

Getting the Daily 411

Now look at the cupboards with your everyday dishes and glasses. Are your dishes chipped and tired? Are your glasses mostly empty jelly jar specials? Is it time for a change? Large home stores sell inexpensive, complete sets of dishes for four. Drinking glasses in all sizes are in the same department. Is it time to add new dishes or glasses to your shopping list?

What about pots and pans? Are yours from a top-of-the-line manufacturer, or did you inherit them from Grandma when you got your first apartment? Of course it's the condition that matters, not the origin. If yours are in bad shape, add a basic set to your current shopping list or, at the very least, create a wish list your family members can use when your birthday rolls around again.

Appliances and Gadgets

Are you an active cook with lots of equipment? Get rid of anything that is rusted, outdated, not working, or simply taking up space. If anything in this purge is going because you're tired of it but it's in great condition, consider donating it to a charity. If anything needs to be fixed, haul it out and take it to a repair shop. Now is the time!

What about the prep items you have? What condition are your bowls in? What about your measuring cups? Anything else in your cabinets that relates to food prep needs to have your honest evaluation.

How many gizmos and gadgets do you need on your counter? Do you have that KitchenAid super mixer on your counter because you're proud you own it, or because you use it every day? What about that juicer that's bigger than your microwave? Do you use it every day, or was that last year's fad? These items need to be tucked away (or given away) if they aren't used regularly. They are space hogs.

When I cooked and had regular dinner parties, my food processor was on my counter. It was like an old friend. I couldn't imagine hauling it out every few days. These days, it's tucked away and makes only guest appearances. Be realistic about your appliances and which ones you use daily. Every kitchen counter is laid out differently to reflect how you use it.

As we progress through life, we inevitably inherit huge, albeit useful, things like the family roasting pan, in which holiday birds and hams have been cooked to perfection for generations. You know the one I'm talking about. Usually it's given to you as a hint that it's your turn to start hosting family gatherings. The problem is, we use them only once or twice a year—and the rest of the time, they take up a huge amount of space.

If you have a garage, attic, basement, or perhaps closet in the dining room that could accommodate a new high shelf, wrap that roasting pan and store it there. Do this, of course, only if you don't have the space in your kitchen. If not, you will frequently find a deep cabinet above the refrigerator. It's high and difficult to access: the perfect resting place for Grandma Mae's magic pan and anything else you'll use rarely.

Hidden Away for Another Day

One of the most difficult kitchen challenges for many people is organizing their storage containers. They usually live in a deep cabinet or drawer—lids and bottoms of various sizes in a random jumble. Take a minute to play matchmaker. In this case, the lonely singles can be tossed out. Only couples need apply.

How about your towels, dishcloths, potholders, and aprons? Are they ancient, stained, crusty? If necessary, add new ones to your shopping list—but don't toss the old ones until you have the new ones! I don't want you to get dirty, have wet hands, or burn yourself because you haven't gone shopping yet!

Most people also have a spot for their sealable bags, foil, wax paper, plastic wrap, and any other form of wrap'n'store you can imagine. Be sure you have what you need and use. If you have a separate pantry or a shelf in the garage or laundry area with household supplies, take the excess there. Like a good surgeon, you want only the scalpel you need at your fingertips.

The Darkest Recesses

Finally, we're going to dive into that area I lovingly call "The Black Hole of Calcutta": that dark, dank, cluttered space under the sink. Once again, discard anything that is old, expired, rusty, or leaking something foul. If you have more than one open bottle of a cleaner, see if you can combine them.

> **Perilous Pitfalls**
>
> If you keep cleaners and household pest poisons under the sink, do not keep any edible food here, including pet food, potatoes, or onions. If appropriate, keep a childproof lock on this cabinet door.

If you have any other areas or categories in your kitchen, take the time you need to weed out the useless, the no longer used, and the outdated. You know who the usual suspects are by now. It's survival of the fittest from this point on.

Gourmet Meal or Take-Out?

No matter the size of the kitchen, the depth of the pantry, or the number of cupboards, it all comes down to one crucial question: *What do you intend to do here?* If you're an amateur gourmet cook, your gastronomic life will get a new lease the minute we get you clutter-free and organized.

If all you do is eat cereal and order take-out, we'll get you set up for one of two occurrences: you marry someone who likes to cook, or your mom will know where to find things when she comes to visit. The process is the same. The number and variety of items staying grows or diminishes in direct proportion to how much you use this room.

Who knows? One day this organized, clutter-free kitchen may inspire the water boiler in you to start cooking.

Create Optimum Work Zones

The traditional way to set up a kitchen is to create work zones. You want to be able to grab everything you need when you are cooking, baking, or storing food without wasting time and energy. This means syncing up your cupboards and drawers so that what you use is close to where you use it. Remember the meat grinder that sat next to the rolling pin? They each need their own space.

You may be asking yourself why you didn't set the kitchen up this way to start. The answer is simple. Most kitchens are unpacked quickly and things get tossed into cupboards and drawers at random. Your immediate goal at the time was to empty the boxes. Now you're seizing the opportunity to make this a room in which you can work with ease—which, by the way, equals more productivity. Let's take a look at our zones.

Traditional Placement

Keep in mind that everyday dishes and glasses are ideally placed in the upper cupboards to the left and right of the sink. Cooking tools generally go in the lower units or cupboards. If this isn't how you have your kitchen set up, take a moment to pull out all the items that relate to each category. Keep them together in one area.

I presume you have a kitchen or dining room table nearby and have a work surface cleared for today. If no table is available, perhaps you have or could borrow a simple card table. Whatever surface you have, be sure to cover it so you don't scratch it.

Prep Zone

I have broken out "prep" as a separate category, although it's technically part of the bigger heading of "cooking." What you have in this category reflects your interest in cooking. You may have lots of tools and aids, or you may be able to skip this category altogether.

"Prep" is short for preparation. Pots and pans are your basic cooking tools. You might be partial to a famous brand like All-Clad or Calphalon. Perhaps you combine those with Pyrex or CorningWare items.

Most of us have a cast iron skillet. Maybe you are an experienced cook and have an adventurous item like a clay roaster in the mix. All of these will be kept together so when you want to cook something, your world of choices is before you.

Before you toss in that pot roast or favorite fish, however, you're going to be busy preparing the entire meal. The items you use are your prep tools. The array is vast and again will depend on your interest level in cooking; however, here are a few basics just about all of us have. Some will be kept in a cupboard while others will be small enough to live in a drawer.

Big Stuff:	**Drawer Dwellers:**
Colander	Potato Peeler
Mandoline	Garlic Press
Food Processor	Thermometer
Mixing Bowls	Cheese Grater
Nut Chopper	Wooden Spoons and/or Spatulas
Timer	Whisks (sizes vary)
Measuring Cups	Measuring Spoons
Pasta Fork	
Large Ladle	

How many of these do you have? Traditionally, these tools are kept near your sink area. The prep phase of cooking involves peeling, chopping, mixing, and cleaning the work surface and our hands. I would begin by looking at the current location of the tools that fall into this category. Perhaps they are grouped and perfectly placed. The typical home cook needs one or two cupboards and one or two drawers near the sink.

Cooking Zone

Most people already have their pots and pans as close to the oven as possible. It's best if you can lay them out flat in the cabinet with their lids in place. If you have to stack your pots, there are holders specifically made for lids that might assist you. If you have space for a hanging pot rack, you've struck gold.

Now check the drawers on either side of the oven or stove. Here you can keep the potholders and tools to use with the pots on the stove. If you like the look, you can always have a pretty ceramic pitcher on or near the stove that holds the tools you use most often, such as wooden spoons, spatulas, a whisk, and so on.

You'll probably discover that you have large serving items you use only for parties or holiday gatherings. I'm thinking of a spaghetti platter with matching bowls or large platters for hors d'oeuvres. Storage of these items will depend on how often you use them. If you feed a large family each night, keep these in a low cupboard near your stove. If they only come out for holidays, tuck them in a high cupboard like the big one over the refrigerator. If they are particularly festive, see if you can put them on display either in the dining room hutch or in a glass-front cupboard in your kitchen.

Baking Zone

If you have young children, you might love helping the little ones make cookies and muffins. You probably have cookie sheets, muffin pans, and the like. These all need to live in a cabinet, and the location depends on the frequency of use. In a typical kitchen, the stove is opposite the sink. Your prep items are in cabinets near the sink, as are your cleanup and storage items. Baking items should be closer to the oven.

If you are a serious cook and baker, there may be items (measuring spoons or measuring cups) you want to duplicate so you can designate them for specific use. For the average cook, this is not necessary. In any event, use duplicates only if you have the cabinet or drawer space to store them.

Perhaps you have a few cookie cutter shapes. If you have just a few, you can easily tuck them into the baking tool drawer. If you have a lot, toss them in a plastic bag and keep them with the baking pans. If they're seasonal, pack them away with your holiday decorations.

Cleanup and Storage Zone

Even if you rarely cook, I'm sure you have plastic bags, plastic wrap, and foil. You want these in a drawer close to those storage containers you matched up with their lids during the initial sweep of the kitchen.

If you rarely cook or have leftovers, you can store your containers up high, but keep the foil and the bags in a drawer close to the sink. There always seems to be a need for these items. And if you use a variety of storage wraps, try not to overload the drawer with too many kinds. Less is more when it comes to decluttering. You'll hear me say this in every room of the home.

The Refrigerator: The Cold, Hard Truth

Is your refrigerator too small for your family? I know this is a big-ticket item, as I had to purchase a refrigerator myself a few years ago. Size, however, is a key issue. Isn't it always?

One way to work this issue, if you have the space, is to put a second refrigerator in the garage. Another trick, if your refrigerator is the right size but you want to buy in quantity to save money, is to put a large freezer in the garage. Of course, these are solutions for folks with large families and their own homes. As a single woman, I wouldn't know what to do with two refrigerators and a big freezer!

Mumbo Jumble

Refrigerators and freezers are frequently a jumble. No one likes clean-up and storage, so everybody rushes, shoving everything in the fridge wherever it fits. We know where the eggs and the butter go because the manufacturer traditionally gives them their own spaces. After that, we're lost.

Let's see if we can make this situation better. Guess what we need? That's right: zones and maintenance. Food doesn't last forever in the refrigerator *or* the freezer. Lots of items, like milk, juices, cheeses, and leftovers, have to be checked regularly. Pick a regular fridge-check time that's logical for your schedule. The night before you make up your shopping list and shop for food is perfect. When you put food in the freezer, by the way, be sure to label and date it.

The Inner Workings

What do you keep in your refrigerator? Can you tell me by category? Here are my departments: dairy, fresh produce, staples (butter, eggs, condiments), whatever I get to cook for that week, and of course any leftovers generated from those meals.

Every category should live in one area of your refrigerator. Here's a peek into my world: I keep dairy and juices on my top shelf and produce in the drawers earmarked for it. Butter is in the door and eggs are on the second shelf with whatever I'm planning to eat that week. (Sometimes I put them in the egg tray; it depends on how quickly I'm planning to use them.) The few condiments I have are in the door.

All meat products go on the bottom shelf. I always know where to look for an item and how much I have of any category.

Decide how to organize your refrigerator after you figure out the diversity and size of your categories. If you're a soda drinker, you can use a beverage can dispenser from The Container Store; it holds a dozen cans. You can also find bacon, hot dog, and butter holders; freezer baskets to help you organize frozen foods; and even a special container to help your baking soda stay fresh and do the same for your refrigerator. Most refrigerators come with a drawer for storing cold-cuts and other meats. Take advantage of all amenities your refrigerator model offers.

Magnetize Me

A refrigerator covered with miscellaneous photos, menus, school notices, and coupons is a visual mess that makes me personally crazy. I frequently use several phrases throughout this book, but none more than "less is more." Look at what's on your refrigerator. If you can't see the refrigerator, it's too much!

In the chapter on paper, we talk about keeping track of school and work schedules. We're searching for ways the whole family can stay in touch without trying to find the pertinent schedule through the paper maze on the door. Photos belong in albums or frames. *Too many magnets spoil the door!* I'm sorry, I couldn't resist.

Perilous Pitfalls

In an emergency, you don't want to scramble for the key phone numbers in your life. Put a list on the refrigerator. If you use your computer, you can update it periodically. Laminate it, if possible.

If you're the parents of young children and have babysitters, it *is* good to have emergency contact numbers listed on a single sheet and posted on the refrigerator door. I would have it laminated. In this age of programmable phones, be sure to program critical numbers into your home phone.

A True Wish List

Finally, your shopping list is the key to keeping your inventory organized and your forays to the grocery store as efficient as possible. If storage space is an issue, in your cupboards or your fridge, you may have to sneak in an extra trip each week to replace perishables, but one trip should be sufficient for the average family.

If you create a master shopping list on your computer for the basic food items you shop for, you can print a fresh one each week. You can group the items either by category (dairy, fruits and veggies, meat and poultry) or by store. This list is one of the few things I think belong on your refrigerator.

Let's Look in Your Drawers

Have you ever had the experience of putting things away in a drawer and then *never seeing them again?* Well, two wonderful products will keep your drawers organized and make it much easier to find whatever you need.

The first item is a drawer liner. I'm not a fan of contact paper myself, but if you prefer that, by all means, use it. Believe it or not, you can use different liners in different drawers. If you like to see a pattern or a color, select one that blends with your kitchen (or whatever room you're organizing). If you're a purist, use one in off-white in all the drawers of your home.

The liner I prefer can be cut to fit the drawer. It's got the consistency of a thick paper towel and, best of all, it's washable. I suggest that you also line the shelves of your cupboards where you have your dishes and glasses. You'll want to purchase a good supply because this liner works beautifully in all the drawers of your home, especially the bathroom.

Another inexpensive organizing tool at your disposal is small containers you can put in your drawers. They come in acrylic, wood, plastic, and mesh. Purchase a variety of containers, and mix and match depending on the sizes you need in each drawer.

In some drawers, you may want to use several containers and then leave a few inches on the side for extra-long items like BBQ tools or wooden spoons. Special junk-drawer organizers are sold separately, but you can make your own by mixing and matching individual containers. Choose whatever method suits you. Of course, one container I do suggest is the silverware caddy. It should fit in one of the top drawers close to the sink and your dishes.

Counters: No More Dumping

When I come home from the store, I unpack my groceries in the kitchen. Perishables go into the refrigerator as I pull them out of the paper or plastic sacks. The other items can be unpacked, sorted, and put away. Don't leave them on the table "for later"! Following through on these tasks right away will keep the clutter from returning. Chores aren't just for kids!

By the way, one of the clutter culprits you can immediately eliminate is extra packaging. For example, when you buy four rolls of toilet paper, typically each roll is wrapped and then all four are packaged in a clear wrap. Toss that clear wrap. Look for extra wrap and cardboard with every purchase and get it out of your home ASAP. Empty those grocery bags and get rid of the excess. No one needs every plastic or paper bag that comes into the home. Keep a small stash in a designated spot so every family member knows where to look. Why not buy a few large canvas shopping bags and help save a few trees? If you have a dog in the home, you can recycle those plastic bags on your daily walks!

What Belongs on the Counter

Set up your counters with the items you use on a regular basis. Every-thing related to one task should be kept close together. That's a sneaky way of saying create categories! For example, I have coffee in the morn-ing. My mugs are on the bottom shelf of a top cabinet near the sink.

Below them on the counter are my coffee bean grinder, purified water pitcher, and coffeemaker. I also have my toaster in this area. Every time you save steps, you save time—time you could be using to make money or have fun.

Keep all the elements of every category you create in the same area. If I used sugar, artificial sweetener, or powdered creamer, for example, I'd have them on a shelf above the mugs or in serving containers on the counter next to my coffeemaker.

In the chapter on dining rooms, we talk about how to store fine china. If yours is packed away but you miss seeing it between holidays and family celebrations, why not use the creamer and sugar bowl from the set? Your morning coffee or tea now has a special touch.

These categories aren't carved in stone, mind you. In the summer months, when the weather is blistering, I like to make fruit smoothies every day, so my blender lives on the counter. In the winter, it's in the back of my tool cabinet. Always be willing to look at the physical life on your counters with fresh eyes.

Mail Call

In the average home, the mail gets dumped on the kitchen counter. If this were temporary, it wouldn't be significant, but it often collects and piles higher and higher. I'm going to suggest some ways to handle this material. The biggest factor is your commitment to deal with it daily.

I suggest you do two things to keep the counter clear: first, open the mail *immediately*. Toss what you don't need. For example, I need my credit card statement and perhaps the return envelope (if you pay online, toss the envelope). I don't need the ads that were stuck inside to tempt me. Toss all junk mail immediately.

Second, take what remains to where you will deal with it. Of course, a home office is ideal—take your bills to your desk and the magazines and catalogs you'll read later to your living room or other favorite read- ing spot. It's also okay to have a decorative basket or other container on the counter to hold the mail, books, and magazines until you take them to your office. Just be sure it's not too big and you empty it *daily*. The important thing is for the kitchen to be dedicated to food preparation and enjoyment, not family business. Those bills aren't going to help your digestion.

Office Corner

If you have a newer home, you may have a nook built into the kitchen with a space from which Mom can run the business of the home. You'll be able to employ many of the office-organizing tips here so that this area stays tidy.

Visuals can affect us more than we realize. If you're preparing dinner and keep seeing that messy stack of unpaid bills and unread magazines out of the corner of your eye, you'll be exhausted before dinner is served. That's one of the reasons clutter is so costly. It wears us out!

Kiddie Korner

Young children always want to do for themselves. It's how they learn and build self-esteem. Most homes with kids have nonbreakable melamine cups, bowls, and dishes with popular cartoon characters on them. Why not use part of one shelf in a low cupboard for these items so that your kids can help themselves?

As they get old enough to feed themselves simple foods like juice and cereal, why not keep those items down low as well? While the kids are developing their self-sufficiency, you'll be saving steps and time. As they get even older, you can have a little step in the kitchen so they can wash those cups and bowls themselves.

Where's the Pantry?

For most of us, especially those living in big-city apartments, the "pantry" is usually a few shelves in a cupboard. When I was growing up in Brooklyn, my mom purchased a freestanding cabinet and used that to supplement her pantry space.

Whatever your setup, keep your food divided by type. For example, here are the most common categories I use. I divide food this way whether I have a client in New York City with two cupboards or a client in Beverly Hills with a walk-in pantry.

- Breakfast foods and cereals
- Snacks (candy, pretzels, cookies)
- Sodas
- Water
- Carbohydrates (rice and pasta)
- Canned vegetables, including pasta sauce
- Canned fruits
- Baking goods (flour, sugars, chocolate pieces)
- Condiments

The key to keeping your pantry in order is to keep these categories separated and organized. There are some great products to assist you. My favorite is a wonderful item called a shelf divider. It's made to slip on a wooden shelf and keep sweater stacks from imploding. I use these here to keep my food categories separated.

When cans sit on a shelf, you can see only the ones in front, right? If you have a cabinet organizer, you will instantly have three levels and all of your cans will be visible. These organizers create graduated levels and come in set widths and expanding versions. They can be made of acrylic, wood, or mesh. There are deep ones for those big cans of beans and very narrow ones to help you organize your spices. Choose whatever looks best in your kitchen.

Deep Thoughts on Cavernous Cupboards

A few things I see in kitchens always make me wonder what the builder had in mind. Do you have cupboards that extend far to one side? A deep pocket like that always looks great until you realize that anything you put back there can be retrieved only by moving just about everything else in the cupboard. Store rarely used items here, perhaps that holiday roasting pan or the cake pans from the baking career you hope to revive one day. You get the idea. It's really wasted space.

You might want this to be the cabinet that holds all your equipment with those less frequently used pieces in the back. Many kitchens have a cabinet with a built-in lazy Susan. This is a great place to store your equipment if you have a lot. If you have only a few pieces, it might share the space with your prep items.

Sometimes a cupboard has extremely deep shelves, and at first you think that's a gift as well. It probably means, however, that

Timely Tidbits

Built-ins and upgrades to the kitchen increase the value of your home when it comes time to sell. You don't have to gut the entire room; you can work in stages. The Container Store will help you space-plan for free.

you'll have to get down on your knees to pull out anything from the back. What to do? Convert to pull-out shelves. This can be done in concert with a full kitchen remodel, or you can do the conversion with a cabinet maker or with portable inserts from The Container Store.

You want to use all the available space in your kitchen to make life easier. If you have high shelves, be sure to use them, even if it's only for storage. Tuck a small step stool in a corner, and you'll have instant access. If reaching for a pot or a mixing bowl becomes a drama because they're difficult to reach, you either stop using them or become so frustrated that the entire meal-preparing experience is a nightmare. Decluttering opens the space so you can use it with ease.

A Spicy Affair

Whether it's 1 spice or 50, we all have some ingredients that spice up our food. Storing them offers a multitude of choices, with one caveat: after six months, any spice will lose its kick, and you don't want to hasten the process by storing them too close to the heat of the stove. Nearby keeps them handy and safe. The most common places for storage are in a spice rack on the counter, in spice jar holders in a drawer, on a shelf, on a shelf creator (the small version of the one I suggested for canned food), or on a lazy Susan on a shelf in a cupboard.

Count your spices and see how many you really use. Let the number dictate what solution you think works best in your kitchen. If you decide to use something on the counter, make sure it adds to the appearance of your kitchen.

All This and the Kitchen Sink

I don't think I've ever been in a home where the area under the sink wasn't a nightmare. It just seems like a great place to stick every miscellaneous item in the kitchen. Let's see if we can make this work in concert with the rest of the room.

In the quick fix at the start of your day, you eliminated and combined. Now, let's take a look at what really should be stored here and how we can keep it together.

What Really Belongs Here?

Once I saw pots and pans stored under the sink. I must say that was an interesting idea. The kitchen in question had deep drawers on either side of the stove, and they were designed for the pots and pans. I understand that in certain parts of the country, this area is the traditional pot-storing place. Let's move yours, however, so that we have this area for more pertinent items.

On the sink proper, I like to have hand soap and dish soap. You can invest in lovely containers or use something you buy at the supermarket. In today's kitchen, I generally see refillable containers being used so the large source containers can logically be stored underneath the sink. Again, as you need more, you won't have to go anywhere to get your supplies, and you'll save time and steps.

You'll be scouring pots and pans here and keeping the kitchen clean. Store all the household cleaners you need in this room under the sink. You can get a two-tier unit to create more space or you can put frequently used items in a caddy. The latter is my favorite solution. Even though you may have only the cleaners you use in this room here, being able to take most everything out at one time will save you time when the plumber comes to call or you spring a leak and have to shut off the water source.

In addition to cleaners, you may have household pest poisons stored here and some plant supplies like a watering can and vitamins for the leafy members of your household. Some people also store the kitchen garbage bags here. If you want to keep paper and plastic grocery bags here, pick a small number and stick to that supply. You don't need to save every single bag that comes home with you.

Keeping It All Safe: Proper Storage and Locks

It is so important to keep small children and animals safe in your home. If either are present, keep a secure lock on the under-sink door. In the best of all possible worlds, while your children are toddlers and into serious exploration of their worlds, you should store all cleaners and poisons on a high shelf. I realize this may not be possible, so do invest in that lock.

Fifi and Fido

I like to see pets have their own area for the food they eat. If you use canned dog food, a shelf creator and a section in a cabinet or the pantry will make Fido's life easier. The same holds true for Fifi the cat. If you use kibble and you purchase it in a large bag, I personally love the new plastic containers on wheels. I keep mine in the kitchen. I have clients who keep them in the pantry area. Some even keep the food right by the door that enters the home from the garage.

> **Timely Tidbits**
>
> Ants will not cross water. If you want to keep your pet food in bags, during warm weather when ants are more likely to invade your home, you can place your container of food on a large tray meant to catch water under a plant. Put about ½ inch of water in the tray and voilà! Your food is safe.

Aftermath

Whether you needed to pull everything out and start over or simply move a few things around, your kitchen should now be ready to serve you. Cooking can be a pleasant experience, whether you're making toast and coffee or preparing a five-course meal.

There's a very easy way to maintain the order you have established, especially if several people in the home use this room and/or you entertain frequently and are blessed with guests who like to help put things away. What is it? Put labels on the shelves and in drawers. Electronic label makers print laminated labels in seconds. You won't find the rolling pin with the meat tenderizer if the drawer simply says "Baking Tools." Best of all, you can use your label maker all over the home to help keep order.

The Least You Need to Know

◆ Every item in the kitchen needs to have a designated spot.

◆ Maintaining the new system takes as much time as maintaining the chaos it's replacing.

◆ All poisonous materials must be kept away from the reach of small children and pets.

◆ No matter what challenges you face in your kitchen, there are tools in the marketplace that will make your space more functional and user-friendly.

5

Dining Room: Does Anyone Eat Here Anymore?

In This Chapter

- ◆ Clear the debris from your dining room
- ◆ Move items abandoned here to their proper place
- ◆ Organize, store, or pass along family treasures
- ◆ Create a space that welcomes family and friends

One of the saddest things I see in most homes is a dining room table covered in debris. Looking for a newspaper from the past two weeks (or longer)? Wonder what Johnny's teacher sent home with him from school last Monday? Thinking of starting a home-based business? Looking for that overdue electric bill? Everything your heart desires has been dumped here. Just don't think about eating a meal, because there ain't no room!

When the next big holiday rolls around, someone in the family usually gets some empty boxes and quickly shovels the contents of the table into them. This stack of boxes (there is rarely just one) gets shoved into the nearest closet. If you're lucky, it will all be looked at again in a few days. In most cases, an unconscious decision is made: the boxes will be abandoned.

The dining room is the space in your home set aside for the family to eat their evening meal together. It's where our extended families and friends gather for holiday and special meals. Even if you dine there as a family only once a week because everyone has such crazy schedules, the room should be ready to accommodate you at a moment's notice.

Assessment

The average dining room suffers from the previously described debris. In addition, I frequently find a hutch, buffet, or sideboard crammed full of "stuff." Sadly, that stuff isn't always dishes and serving pieces. Have you shoved anything into your hutch lately? Sometimes I find enough dishes to serve several large families in style. What's in *your* hutch?

The debris in your dining room is unique to your family size and life-style. For some readers, their children's toys may be scattered around the floor, not to mention the dog's latest chew toy or bed. Are you into crafts? Have the pieces for your next project been waiting on the dining room table for you to get started? How many months has it all been there?

Tailor-Made

For our purposes, the dining room we're decluttering is a separate room. Feel free to tailor the instructions to your personal situation. For example, I have a dining area off my kitchen that opens into my living room. I have a table, four chairs, and a hutch.

Last fall, just before I painted and had new carpet installed, I took stock of my own situation. My days of dinner parties are in the past. I moved my dining room furniture into a corner of the living room. My official dining room space now has a new love seat, a matching ottoman, two side tables, and lamps. I begin the day here with the newspaper and my morning coffee. It was a daring move and shocked many of my friends. This action transformed the dining area into one I use every day instead of one I enjoyed one or two nights a year with guests. Do you need to shake up the furniture arrangement in your dining room?

Take Stock

Have a seat in the dining room. Be sure to have your *Declutter Notebook* with you. What's preventing you from eating and entertaining here? Jot down a list of things that cause the current chaos, using the previous descriptions as a guide. Be as specific as you can. You don't have to write down your feelings, just a simple, concrete list of the issues. After you identify the problems, you can begin to solve the issues that created them.

Some Tools Make Light Work

Since the clutter is leaving today, you'll need a good supply of sturdy trash bags. Perhaps you'll need a box or two to transport papers or craft supplies to your office or work area. If you must use this area for homework or crafts, you may need special containers to house your supplies.

If you decide you want to protect your good china and crystal before storing it, there are containers made for this purpose. We'll be looking at the two best choices in a minute.

You may not want to pack your china away because you want to be able to grab a plate or cup at will. Perhaps you use your fine china more often than the average person. In this case, consider some plate separators. These are large soft squares of heavy felt that keep a stack of dishes from touching. They really help prevent scratches.

After you gather your basic supplies, remember to set aside a specific time to declutter.

The Quick Fix

Take care of the following before we begin:

◆ Take items that belong in other rooms there now. (Do not stop in those rooms to start decluttering!) Stack or place the new additions neatly and return immediately to the dining room.

◆ All items that you recognize as trash should be placed in trash bags.

> **Perilous Pitfalls**
>
> You can lose precious time by starting decluttering projects in multiple rooms. Working in several areas or rooms at one time splinters your focus and makes you feel tired. Take one step at a time to success.

◆ Set aside anything that belongs to someone else, preferably near the front door. These things should exit your home as quickly as possible.

◆ Too much furniture and too many knick-knacks, serving pieces, and dishes make a room feel crowded and uninviting. Is it time to donate some to a relative or a charity?

When Paper Eats the Dining Room Table

Papers wind up on the dining room table because they haven't been assigned a designated spot in your home. This was the default position. You need to set up a file system to properly house them. Setting up a working file system is an art that we tackle in detail in Chapter 10.

In the meantime, take a minute to place the collected stack(s) of papers in a box for transport to your office proper or current work area in the home. As you do this, see if you can toss anything immediately. Examples include old newspapers and magazines, junk mail, outdated papers from your child's school, invitations to parties that have already taken place, flyers for the supermarket, expired coupons, department store sales long past, and more.

Dining Room Darlings: Buffets and Hutches

In keeping with the theme for this room, the hutch, sideboard, or buffet, the furniture pieces traditionally used in this room, are meant to house serving and display items only. Most of us have everyday dishes in the kitchen. If we're lucky, we've either purchased, inherited, or been given a set of good china. This is the perfect place to house that set.

When the dining room table is cleared off, you can use it as a worktable for decluttering your hutch or cupboard. Be sure to cover it so you don't scratch it in the process. Let's begin by dividing the items in this room into categories. The most likely categories for this room are as follows:

- Special-occasion pieces (china, crystal, fine linens, and so on)
- Large serving pieces
- Items classified as antiques and/or display-only pieces

Does this sound like your dining room? Let's put one entire category on the table at a time, starting with the fine china.

Pampered Plates and Friends

The traditional way to store china and crystal is in soft zippered pouches, with each item separated by a divider. Today there are also storage boxes. Since the furniture pieces in this room were designed to house china sets, you should have no trouble placing your containers here for the set you want to keep in this room. Personally, I would use the pouches for storage in your dining room furniture and consider the boxes for any sets you keep elsewhere. The choice is yours.

Here, Darling, This Is for You ...

If you have "good china" from several family members, it can be more of a curse than a blessing. Ask yourself some questions about these sets: do you use the same set for all holidays and special occasions, or do you switch off for variety? If you do stick with one, is it time to give the other sets to a family member? Could you sell one on eBay or place it with an antique dealer?

It's the rare dining room that holds enough furniture to accommodate multiple sets of china. If you aren't ready to part with your extra set, pack it away and store elsewhere if necessary. Don't forget that you can put one or two pieces from the set on display in your hutch.

Isn't It Lovely?

Remember that you want to keep the good china you actually use handy. If it moves to the garage, the attic, or some other faraway location, it's going to be a pain in the neck to retrieve it. Many people like to have an entire set on display in their hutch. I used to be of this mind-set. And then I lived through the Northridge Earthquake in California.

The dishes I inherited from my mother came crashing to the floor. One minute they were my treasures, the next they were literally my trash. Now my good dishes are tucked away in my hutch in nicely padded containers. An ounce of prevention is indeed worth a pound of cure.

How It Sparkles and Shines

Let's move on to the crystal. Set it out on the dining room table and consider the guidelines you used to sort through your dishes. Do you need all of it? Do you use any of it regularly? You may already have or may consider purchasing a small display cabinet for your crystal. These are usually tall, narrow pieces and are frequently made for a corner. Often there is lighting inside. Remember, you want to display select items, not everything you own—especially if you have been collecting for years.

What Did I Have Again?

Before you pack any items away, be sure to photograph the china and crystal if it's insured. In the event of a theft or natural disaster, you can use this documentation to file a claim. By the way, as you pack them away, take this opportunity to toss your chipped dishes and glasses. It may be true that Grandma Mae used them, but no guest is going to be thrilled to. Remember Grandma Mae with the good care you are taking of the items that survived.

Set a Pretty Table

Dining room furniture traditionally has several drawers. Here is the ideal place to store the antique or high-quality linens you may have inherited or purchased for entertaining, as well as the good silverware.

Special sterling silver storage cloths will keep the need to polish to a minimum.

Most top drawers in the hutch are designed for silverware and have dividers built in. You can have a cabinetmaker do the same for you if needed, or you can use drawer liners and insert containers as we did in the kitchen.

If you have the drawer space, you may also want to keep napkin rings, candles, and other small items you use to dress your table here. I like to use china name cardholders with my place settings. What treasures do you use to make your table festive and unique?

From time to time, many of us use tablecloths in the dining room. After they are returned from the cleaners, some can pose a storage problem. It's okay to leave them on the extra thick hangars they are sent home on; remove the plastic and allow the garment to breathe.

Make space in the closet closest to the dining room. If necessary, you can cover them with a sheet. Plastic seals in the chemicals the linens were cleaned with and can pose a health risk. Ideally, if they aren't too bulky, they will fit in the bottom (traditionally long) drawer of your hutch.

Perilous Pitfalls

Fine linens can be damaged if you leave them in the dry cleaner's plastic bags. The plastic seals in the chemicals used to clean the fabric. In addition, moisture can break down and stain fine linen when it's sealed in plastic.

Let It All Hang Out—at Different Times

Whether you have a hutch with a display top or a sideboard with a large, flat surface, be sure the items you place here are special and add personality to the room. If you have a lot of things, why not rotate them with the seasons? This rotation will prevent you from getting bored with your own display. It also gives you the opportunity to enjoy more prized possessions over the course of a year. Remember, too, that some of your display items may look lovely

Timely Tidbits

When you rotate the decorative items you have on display, guests and family members often think you have redecorated. We sense something is different, yet we can't quite put our finger on exactly what it is.

elsewhere in your home. Of course, I am thinking more about your antiques than I am imagining a spare place-setting on the coffee table. Enjoy what you own rather than packing most of it away.

I frequent a post office where one of the postal clerks loves to decorate her cubicle for the seasons. She covers every square inch of her space. She goes so overboard that her colleagues do absolutely nothing—for self-preservation, I am sure. At Christmas it looks as if two prison inmates are working next to a psychotic elf on speed. When you dress up this room with your treasures, remember, "less is more." Less is also easier to dust.

When It's Time to Say Farewell

If you're in the process of downsizing, you may feel it's time to let your children or grandchildren inherit the fine dishes, crystal, linens, and antiques that have graced your life. The process of decluttering is the perfect time to give these gifts. You'll still get to enjoy these items on holidays, but now it won't be up to you to set the table, wash the dishes, and store everything for next time.

Conversely, if you are living in a small space like a studio, for example, and have no place to store the family treasures you have been given, either ask a trusted relative to hold them for you or place them in a secure storage facility. If you have homeowners insurance, it may cover these possessions. Be sure to check. If you don't have insurance, storage facilities will sell you a policy to protect the items you leave with them.

Table Dressing

Now that your room is debris-free, filled with your special entertaining items, and organized, why not make it beautiful and inviting? Here are some ideas to spark your creativity.

- If you have a green thumb and the lighting is right, put a plant in the center of the table.

- Do you have any family heirlooms that would be appropriate here? You can be reminded of Grandma Mae every day.

- Another choice is to use a large serving piece from the set you have on display or tucked away in your hutch.

- Fresh-cut flowers in a beautiful vase are always lovely here.

- You can change your tablecloths or runners with the seasons.

- Candles in beautiful holders are perhaps my favorite choice for the table. Dining by candlelight doesn't have to be exclusively for lovers.

Whatever you decide, keep it simple and in good taste. You've worked hard to make this room inviting for family and friends. Now is the time to enjoy the fruits of your labors. Get accustomed to the openness and beauty of the room just as you were once overwhelmed by its debris and chaos. The next time you dump an armful of miscellaneous stuff on the table, the pretty centerpiece you have carefully chosen is going to look terribly out of place. Maintenance is a matter of daily vigilance.

What About Kids and Crafts?

Sometimes a house or apartment is small and there is no other place for homework and crafts to be done. Ideally, there is space in the family room for crafts, and the children can do homework at the kitchen table or in their room. Life, however, is rarely ideal. With a little imagination, we can multitask in the dining room and still keep it clutter-free and ready for entertaining.

How much furniture do you have in this room? Does it all need to house your china and crystal? For example, your hutch should be the place you store those items. However, you might clear out the sideboard and store craft supplies there. The children can do homework at the table after school; however, the table should be cleared off at day's end. I know this works, as it was the arrangement in our household while I was growing up.

If all of the existing furniture must house china, crystal, service pieces, and so on, you can invest in some portable, inexpensive multidrawer storage containers on wheels for the crafts and homework supplies. Tuck them in a corner of the nearest closet during the day, and wheel them to the table when they are needed. You'll find pictures of these items in Chapter 7.

If you have very young children and you find their toys in every room, teach the kids to return their toys to one or two central areas. Traditionally, these would be their bedroom and/or the family room. When my best friend Susie's little girl was 2, before she came to dinner or went to bed at night, she had to pick up her room. This meant she put books on her bookshelf, soft toys in one container, dolls in another, and stuffed toys on her bed. It's never too early to learn the value of creating and maintaining categories.

Aftermath

A funny thing happens to people who stop before the process of decluttering is over: they inadvertently create more chaos. The very state they were trying to fix gets worse. We've all experienced this, and it's avoidable.

When you are done with your decluttering work in the dining room, don't forget that you may have some loose ends to tie up. Finish the job by finding places for the things you moved out of the dining room. Staying decluttered happens only if you complete each step of the process. Here are some steps to help you stay on top of your new decluttering habits.

◆ Schedule time to shop for additional organizing tools.

◆ Deliver items to a charity and/or schedule a pick-up.

◆ Schedule the return of items to family members and friends who reside outside your home.

◆ Take out the trash and/or recycling materials.

◆ If you took some items to a newly decluttered location during our Quick Fix phase, now is the time to integrate those items into the new system.

◆ If you took some items to areas that are still cluttered, be sure that declutter project has been scheduled on your calendar.

Timely Tidbits

If the dining room table has been your automatic dumping ground, simply do not stop here when you enter your home. This is an example of a good habit you can create for yourself.

Look at it this way: you either take a few minutes each day to put things where they belong in the home, or you can spend a day or two slogging through piles every year or so. Remember the old saying—an ounce of prevention is worth a pound of cure.

The Least You Need to Know

- Less is more in the dining room. Be judicious as you choose what to display and what to store.

- If you need or want to use the dining room in a creative way, such as a craft or homework area, set it up so that those activities can be put away and taken out on an as-needed basis.

- While you may drop things off in the dining room from time to time, at day's end everything must be taken to its designated spot in the home. Daily maintenance is at the heart of an organized, clutter-free space.

Chapter 6

Family Room: Not Just for TV Anymore?

In This Chapter

- Taming those DVDs; CDs; and, if you still have them, VHS tapes and records
- Making today's paper or this month's magazine a moment of pleasure in a busy day
- Helping your children create fun zones
- Deciding what to display for family and friends

I can remember every detail of the living room in our Brooklyn brownstone. The room was frozen in a kind of suspended perfection, waiting to wow guests. The fact that we rarely entertained didn't seem to matter to my mother. The room was ready. In her world, that's what counted. I had friends, on the other hand, who were allowed to play in what we called "rec rooms." This was short for "recreation room," and it meant their parents had turned the basement into a kid-friendly zone.

Time has passed, and while we still have formal living rooms for enter-taining guests, now there is almost always a room in the main part of the house where the family gathers. The rec room has come of age. Recently, I was in a home that has the latest design: the family room opens off the kitchen. There is no wall separating them. The emotional benefits to this room in terms of family connection and unity are enormous.

The potential for physical chaos, however, is probably higher in any room used by everyone in the home. Let's see how we can create a room where we feel comfortable and our friends are welcome without warning. How about that for a tall order?

Assessment: What's Here and What Tools Do I Need?

Enter your family room and have a seat. Have your *Declutter Notebook* and a pen or pencil with you. Relax a minute and just look around. For most people, this room is in turmoil. If that's your situation, relax—you're in good company. Let me tell you my goals for you and this room by sharing a true story.

One day I visited a friend. We were scheduled to go to an event together. I happened to arrive a few minutes early. My friend said she was ready, but she had to pick up the family room before she left. I looked in and thought to myself, "This is going to take hours!" I went to the bathroom to freshen up. I returned less than 10 minutes later and was stunned to see a picture-perfect room. Here is my friend's philosophy—and her secret.

The Speedy Pickup

My friend has several teenage children, and her home is always open to them and their friends. As an organized person, she has established a designated place for everything in her home. If clutter appears, one of three things has to happen: the item gets put away, it's tossed, or it's new and an official spot is appointed. This is what I call having a sys-tem. My friend was working her system that morning. It reminded me how powerful a good system is and how easily it can make a difference.

Fluff and Fold

What if the item is in its place but it has been tossed into a heap? Do you have any throws or big pillows in your family room so folks can curl up, watch a movie, and stay warm? They will look like clutter if they are tossed carelessly onto the floor or the couch. The throws need to be neatly folded and the pillows fluffed and/or piled neatly. Let's say you're watching a movie and during the commercial breaks, you get up for snacks or a bathroom break. Am I suggesting you neatly fold your throw every time? No! But the end of the evening, as you're shutting things down and getting ready for bed, is the perfect time. I want you to live a clutter-free, organized life—I don't want you to become a robot!

The True Age of "Restoration"

My mother taught me how to be a good guest. She said when I walked into a room in a friend's home I needed to take a mental picture. I could relax and enjoy myself, but the room had to be restored when I left. She would say, "Your hosts have decided this is how they want the room to look, and you need to honor that." In the same way, all the members of a family have to work in concert to make their home look and feel good, for their enjoyment as well as that of family and friends. If Mom is doing all the picking up, chores need to be assigned.

So here's my question: if you set a timer for 10 minutes, could you restore the room to order? Or does stuff have no designated place? Worse, is there just too much stuff to begin with? If it's the first scenario, set your timer and get to work. This chapter may yield food for thought, but I would guess other areas of the home are your challenge, not this one. If the latter situations are the case, grab some of those trusty heavy-duty garbage bags. We're about to have a quick fix.

Timely Tidbits

Children should enjoy the family room and be allowed to mess it up while they play. They also need to be responsible for restoring it when playtime is over. This room is full of chore assignments for every member of the family.

The Quick Fix

Let's begin with the easy stuff. We always want to make an immediate visual impression so that we stay motivated. First, go around the room and toss anything that's trash. Then return to other rooms the items that have been left here. I can see you tossing the remnants of last night's movie popcorn and taking the bowl to the kitchen. I see you hanging up jackets and sweaters that got tossed as family members entered the room. Take care of these things first.

Now pause a minute and look around. Notice all the things you could do to make the room look better. Fold those cozy throws, fluff the couch pillows, and pile up those used for extra seating. Put things away in their current designated spots. Let's say, for example, you have all your DVDs in a cabinet under the TV. Put them away and make a note in your *Declutter Notebook* if your storage isn't adequate.

If you don't have a designated spot for some items but they're always in this room, create physical groupings in the room so you see what you have. I'm thinking of toys, board games, craft supplies, and pleasure reading like books, magazines, and newspapers.

Finally, let's look at the groupings. Does every item have to be here? Are there too many toys, for example? Could some be put in your children's rooms? Are some ready to be donated? Before we work on how to display or store what's staying, be honest and see if you really need everything in the groupings you have created.

The Heart of the Home

The kitchen is the commonly designated heart of the home. However, the family room has great potential to rival it. One of the things to notice in this room is how well it has been set up.

+ Is this a cozy, inviting space? If you said "Yes," what makes it that way? If you said "No," what besides the clutter is preventing you from feeling good in this space?

+ Is the lighting adequate?

- Do you have too much furniture, or do you need more? Would pieces in other rooms serve you better here? Or could you move some things out of this room and use them better elsewhere?

- Are there too many decorative items here? Could they migrate to another part of the house, or should some things be packed away, sold, or tossed?

Take a visual inventory. Everywhere you look, you want to be invited into the room to relax and have fun. Is that what your family room communicates now? Take out your notebook and make some notes about items you need to shop for. When you are done with that task, let's continue our work.

On Display

When you go to a movie or play, a set decorator has been at work to silently communicate with you. This person tells you things about the characters using the environment. You do the same in your home. In the family room, we often see evidence of a hobby either one or more people enjoy.

It's wonderful to share your triumphs as a skeet shooter, quiltmaker, golfer, horsewoman, or anything else. The problem arises when we put up something and never take it down. We're too busy adding. When there is too much stuff, the eye doesn't know where to rest. All you have is clutter. You may need to pare. Take a look around and see what this room reveals about your family. Is it the story you want to tell? Remember that photo clutter can be on your walls, not just the flat surfaces.

Let Your Photos Tell a Tale

I have a client who is a doting mother. Her husband died when her children were very young. I had the pleasure of unpacking the family in their new home when they moved to Los Angeles. As often happens, I notice things as an outsider that the parents miss because they are so close to the situation.

In this case, as my team unpacked artwork and photos, we all noticed an inordinate number of formal portraits of the children. It seemed as if every era in their young lives had been documented. The daughter had not changed. I related to that; if you look at my baby pictures, there is my face in miniature. The son, however, had been through a remarkable transformation. As a young child, he was very heavy. Now, as a young man in his late teens, he was reed thin and muscular. I was sure the girls were going to be after him when he entered school in the fall. I was equally sure he was going to cringe every time friends came over to the house and saw large framed photos documenting his chubby youth all over the house. It was more than conjecture on my part, by the way. He kept asking his mom not to hang "those old pictures." Mom didn't understand where that remark was coming from. From her perspective, she wanted everyone who entered the home to see the journey they had taken as a family. All her son saw were pictures of a time he would rather forget.

Timely Tidbits

Display the latest photos on your wall or in frames around the room. Put the oldest photos in albums. Be sure you use acid-free paper to preserve your treasures for the next generation to enjoy.

Do you relate to this story? Do you look around your family room and see a shrine to your children's past, or your own? What story do your photos tell?

Perhaps some formal portraits need to be put away for your children and the homes they will one day create. Perhaps you need to purchase fresh frames, or maybe the photos in your home need to change location. Take some time to craft a creative solution to your photo issue. Be the set decorator in your home.

Is It a Heap or a Hope?

If you have had boxes of photos yet to be put into albums for many, many years, again, take heart and join the majority. There is a quick fix and a real fix to this problem. Sort them in order. The quick fix is to spend an afternoon looking through your photos. Fearlessly toss all those that you realize will never ever go into an album or frame. If you have no order at all to your photos, simply divide them by occasion or holiday. You will wind up with stacks of photos, including many of the following categories:

- Birthday parties
- Chanukah celebrations
- Christenings/baptisms
- Christmas dinners
- Easter celebrations
- Fourth of July parties
- Graduation ceremonies and parties

- Halloween costumes and parties
- School performances
- Sporting events
- Thanksgiving dinners
- Trips

… and whatever other holidays and events your family celebrates.

Then place these in photo storage boxes. There are decorative ones and ones that are meant for long-term archival storage. Decide how long it will be before you have time to make your albums, and choose accordingly. You can find a wonderful selection of both types at stores like Michael's Arts and Crafts, Target, Bed Bath and Beyond, and The Container Store.

The front of each box has a space for you to label the contents. Use your label maker or create them on the computer. I found wonderful storage towers for photos in the Exposures Catalogue (www.exposuresonline. com). Some of the towers hold as many as 10 boxes, which translates to thousands of photos. Instead of a collection of sloppy cardboard boxes and a jumble of photos, you have your "album-making project" sitting in a corner of the family room looking beautiful, organized, and oh-so-clutter-free.

The Digital Age Descends

If you're a totally digital family, remember to save your photos on disks; otherwise, your computer will get bogged down. This also preserves them in case of a hard-drive crash. You can keep the same categories for disk storage/organization that you used for the photos you have developed or printed out. You can also put digital shots into cyber-albums and share them with more family members and friends than their hard-copy counterparts—all with the click of your mouse. I must confess, however, that I'm partial to the old-fashioned form.

Memorabilia

In many cultural and spiritual traditions, it's important to honor and remember the past. I think when we have a personal triumph or rise above adversity, it is indeed important to document that time. A problem arises, however, when we decide that every single item from an era is precious. This can translate to saving every piece of paper we touch on a trip to a foreign country, holding on to every item of clothing a late relative had in the closet, or making the transition to a new job and holding on to the remnants of the former one.

> **Perilous Pitfalls**
>
> Sorting memorabilia and photos can be very difficult emotionally. We run the risk of getting paralyzed and throwing in the towel. Ask an organized friend who has already done this work to sit with you, help you make decisions, and keep you moving.

I see it all the time. Doctors and lawyers hold on to textbooks. Entrepreneurs keep office stationery from business ventures long abandoned. Moms get attached to office material they used at the job they had before they quit the workforce. You get the idea. Look at your memorabilia (which frequently gets stored in this room) and start tossing so that what you wind up with are the true treasures of the past.

You can find beautiful boxes made for holding memorabilia and, as you might imagine, storage towers that will hold the containers. You can coordinate the boxes used for photos and memorabilia with the albums you make. Once you do your sorting, you can get into the creative part of this adventure. You can now have your photos, memorabilia, and completed albums side by side in beautiful pieces of furniture in this room. Why take the time to make an album or create a scrapbook if you never share it with family and friends? This is the ideal room to have your treasures within easy reach.

Newspapers and Magazines

Newspapers and magazines can pile up all over the house. We need to corral them, and this room is a good candidate. Let's talk about categories. All newspapers and magazines are not created equal.

If you have a home office, take your business-related subscription periodicals and newspapers there. I can't imagine that the toddlers in your home care about the *Wall Street Journal* or what the AMA or local Bar Association has to say today! If you have a busy week and just can't read the paper each night, schedule some time on the weekend to peruse and toss. Don't drag last week's news into next week.

> **Timely Tidbits**
> Many business newsletters and periodicals are now available on the Internet. See if your business subscriptions can be delivered to your e-mail inbox. This will cut the paper clutter from your home.

If you like to read fashion magazines before bed because the images are so much fun, put them in your bedroom, but be sure they're in magazine holders. Let's say you're planning a remodel and you are in the picture-collecting phase; it would be nice to have those magazines in the family room.

> **Timely Tidbits**
> If you're collecting magazines for reference or a special project, be sure you don't buy so many magazines that you overwhelm yourself.

By the way, in Chapter 10, on home offices, we examine the best way to set up files. Here's a wonderful example of how files can help you with a home project. Cut your design pictures out of magazines and put them into categories. When I was redecorating last fall, I had the following categories:

- ◆ Bathroom images
- ◆ Bedroom images
- ◆ Furniture
- ◆ Paint
- ◆ Window dressing

Perilous Pitfalls

Piles lead to clutter because anything's hard to find in a stack. Keep things like magazines standing up in holders designed for this purpose. You will never hunt for your favorite issue again.

Instead of stacks of magazines, I had tidy files of my favorite images.

The Container Store and Exposures Catalogue have beautiful holders for magazines and newspapers. It's important to keep items like these from spreading all over a table or the floor. My set is made of a natural fiber called Makati. I was tempted to get the set in bamboo. Search for the type that best serves the overall decorative theme in your home. That's the luxury we have today: containers designed for practical purposes are now made to enhance the décor in a room. We can declutter and beautify in one step!

Music and Movies: That's Entertainment

Today the average person amasses such large collections that it's difficult to find space for everything. The first thing you need to do is sort your treasures. This probably will take some time, so don't start this task unless you have an hour or two. I don't suggest you do this piecemeal; other members of the family might start searching for a specific movie or CD, and then there you are with a pile of clutter and chaos.

The Right Sort

First, sort your collection into the broad categories:

Audio:

♦ CDs

♦ Audiocassettes

♦ Records

Video:

♦ VHS videotapes

♦ DVDs

Once the category creation is complete, take one category at a time into a work area. Is your craft table free? How about the coffee table? The floor will do if you have space to spread out. Let's look at each one and see how we can get it under control.

CDs

This is surely how most of us enjoy our music today. See if you have any that no longer interest you. You can pass these along to a charity or a good friend. For music collections, no matter the format, it's really difficult to keep them in alphabetical order. If you live alone, of course, you won't have a problem. Asking all the members of a large family to honor this system is often difficult. What to do? Divide your collection by type of music: rock, hip-hop, classical, country, and so on. Then physically separate your types. If the kids simply have to put things back in the right category, you are ahead of the game. If they don't comply, give one of them the chore of restoring the categories at the end of the week. Rotate this assignment.

Audiocassettes

If you still play your cassettes, by all means, keep them in the family room. More and more, of course, they are replaced by CDs. If you can, transfer your favorite audiocassettes to CD for uniformity. Are there any you can donate? With all our categories, we want to whittle them down to the realistic few you will continue to enjoy.

Records

Depending on your age, you either have a large collection you treasure or these are museum relics to you. If you're a collector but no longer play them, be sure you store them in special boxes meant to hold records. Do not stack these boxes! You don't want to warp your records and render them unplayable.

If you aren't going to keep them in the family room, it's also important that you store them where they will not be subject to extremes of heat, cold, or, obviously, moisture. By the way, The Container Store has special frames for album covers. Maybe one or two old Beatles records on the family room wall will tickle your fancy?

Music and movies can be stored in various ways. I toss out a few of the most common here. You can mix and match your solutions, depending on the size of your collection, the décor, and the space in your family room. In addition, your solutions need to be in sync with your personality. I am very organized, for example, but I don't want to alphabetize my collections. It strikes me as burdensome. I like the "category separation method." My collections are very small, so retrieval is a snap. If it's easy and fun for you, once a system is in place, you will be able to adhere to it.

Finally, as the children in a family grow older, their collections rival their parents'. Allow them to keep their music and videos separate from the family's general stash. Talk to them about the various ways to organize their collections, and then let their creativity reign. Remember that getting organized is partially developing a skill and partially being creative. If you make tasks like this fun for your children, they will want to be organized in other areas of their lives, like in those "famous" rooms they sleep in every night!

Following are some ideas for music and movie storage.

The Wall Unit

If you have a wall unit, devote some of your shelves to your collections. Keep your selections standing upright either by having them extend across an entire shelf or by using a bookend.

If you can, hire a carpenter to install pull-out drawers in an existing cupboard or built-in unit. This will showcase your collection at a glance. These work on the same principle as the pull-out shelves I spoke about for the kitchen.

Containers to the Rescue

There are numerous storage containers on the market. These can be put out on the floor, the coffee table, or some shelves. The Container Store's Elfa System has a special adjustable shelving unit that houses VHS tapes and jewel cases with ease. As always, bring in your dimensions and the size of your collections, and they will space-plan your custom unit for free.

My favorite solution is the easiest of all. I use media binders for my CDs and DVDs. I have one in the car and one in my living room.

My collections are always portable and don't take up any space at all. The problem for some clients is what to do with the jewel cases. I toss mine. You may want to box yours and stow them away in the garage or the back of a closet. This way, when you want to trade or sell some, you'll have a complete package.

Perilous Pitfalls

If you keep VHS tapes or CD/DVD jewel cases in rows rather than stacks, be sure to use bookends. If these items are falling over, they will look sloppy and give the room a cluttered appearance—even if they *are* in alphabetical order.

Videotapes and DVDs

One day these tapes were popular; the next, they were eclipsed by DVDs. Technology is amazing, isn't it? You will want to take a realistic look at your collection. Keep movies that you truly treasure and will watch again. Donate the others to a charity. Think how much fun you can bring to those shut in at senior homes, orphanages, or hospitals. If you just can't part with some but know you won't be viewing them, store them elsewhere.

Just as you made music divisions in your music collection, you can do the same here and with your VHS videotapes and DVDs. Divide the whole collection into the following categories:

Timely Tidbits

The trick to bringing order to media collections is twofold: pare them to what you'll really enjoy, and make them accessible.

- ◆ Action-Adventure
- ◆ Classics
- ◆ Comedy
- ◆ Drama
- ◆ Documentary
- ◆ Faith and Spirituality

- ◆ Foreign Films
- ◆ Kid Videos
- ◆ Musicals/Music Videos
- ◆ Romance
- ◆ Sci-Fi/Fantasy
- ◆ Sports/Fitness

Do you have another category? Don't forget to separate those items. I'll bet the teens in the house have a Horror Movie section, don't they?

Timely Tidbits

In addition to a charity, you can host an entertainment swap party where you and your friends trade music and movies in all formats (audiocassettes, CDs, DVDs, VHS).

Once again, these smaller groupings are easier to maintain than having all DVDs (or VHS tapes) in one area, even if they are alphabetized. Now when you are looking for a specific comedy or musical, thumbing through your selection may remind you of another choice you can enjoy on the same night.

When the TV Goes Off ... What Will We Do?

"Family room" means the family gathers here. If everyone just stares mindlessly at the TV or plays video games, however, the room isn't really living up to its full potential. This is a place where games can be played, parties can be held, and conversations should be enjoyed.

In the section "The Heart of the Home," you considered the furniture in this room. Once you have that set, be sure it's arranged so that there are areas for the different kinds of activities this room can entertain. Clutter often develops when we attempt an activity and we aren't set up to accomplish it successfully. For example, when you are taking images out of magazines for research, you'll need scissors, file folders, your label maker, and, of course, a trash can. If you were making a Dream Board, you'd need scissors, glue, your board, and a trash can. Get the idea?

Perilous Pitfalls

Kids will have spills in this room. Going into a panic will make the room seem unfriendly. Be ready with some or all of the following antidotes: have fabric-covered furniture treated for easy cleanup, place coasters liberally about the room, have large sheets of paper to put under craft projects to protect the table (or select a table with a washable surface), and be sure there are enough trash cans to catch everyone's debris.

Wonderful Workspace

Having the supplies and no place to work creates another problem. Look around your family room one more time. Is there a table where craft projects can be worked on? The table Grandma Mae left you with her famous turkey roaster might not be the best choice here if some of your projects are messy. It's nice to have a work surface that's easy to clean and forgiving about things like paint, glue, and glitter.

Set Up for Success

Is there a comfortable reading chair with a good light source for enjoying the books, magazines, and newspapers that are kept here? Where can you set up a board game? Will you use the craft table, or do you have a big coffee table that will do the job? Or perhaps you have a card table tucked into a corner? (It could live in the garage if these two rooms are close.) Do you have enough chairs in this room? Or can you borrow from a nearby room? As with all the rooms, be specific about what you're going to do in this room, and then set yourself up to be successful with ease and no clutter!

"A House Without Books Is Like a House Without Windows"

I grew up with this motto. Sadly, it seems to have passed from daily speech. It's a wonderful way of saying that every home ought to have books—not books for show, but books that are read, savored, and saved like old friends. It's nice to divide your book collection so that a particular category is where you will most need it. You wouldn't search for a cookbook in your bathroom, right? Let's look at the books you have here.

See if you have books that you can donate. Sometimes our books need to move on to the next place where they can make a contribution and be appreciated. Next, divide them into categories. If everyone in the family enjoys this room and likes to read, you might not be able to give everybody their own bookcase, but you can assign shelves. Little ones get the bottom shelves so they can grab their own. Just be sure you ask them to return them when they're done.

Some people like to alphabetize their books. For the average family collection, this may cause more issues than it solves. You're going to be mixing sizes, and the final visual may ironically create the look of clutter. Keep categories together and vary the way the books are placed on the shelf. Alternate the stacks with books that are standing upright and books that are lying down horizontally. This is a nice way to create an area where you can display some of your decorative pieces or a special collection. Your visual will be inviting and tidy.

When the Floor Is Littered with Toys

If your floor is constantly littered with toys, there may be several causes. More than likely, it's a combination of these things. See which you relate to in terms of your children:

♦ My children have mountains of toys. There are so many that it's impossible to create any order.

♦ I ask my children to put their toys away, but they refuse.

♦ I've never asked my children to put their toys away. You're only young once, right?

♦ My kids are willing to pick up their toys, but I don't have anything for them to put the toys into. What kind of storage is best?

How did you do here? Did you relate? Let's look at each one in turn, shall we?

Toy Eliminator

In terms of the first possibility, you know you have to pare the selection. If everything is in great condition, try to rotate the items you have out at any one time. Toys will once again stimulate your children's interest if they haven't seen them in a while. If you want to save things for the next child, store away those toys your older child has already outgrown.

Charity ... It Isn't Just a Tax Deduction

You can use toys to introduce your children to the concept of giving to those who are less fortunate. Take your child with you when you make a toy run to your favorite charity or homeless shelter. Some of my clients have the "for every new toy in, the same number of old toys goes to charity" rule. Their children get very excited at the idea of helping others. You may be surprised by how generous your children can be when they are in control of the giving.

Responsible Kids

If your situation is the second possibility, my question is simple: Why are you asking rather than telling your children to pick up their toys? Children need clear direction. They also need to understand that there are consequences for refusing a parental request. After the first refusal, tell them that the toy in question will be taken away. If they continue to refuse, follow through on your threat and remove the toy. They won't refuse again if they know you are serious. Good behavior is the key to having any confiscated toy returned.

If you think being young means having no responsibility, how and when do you think your children will learn to be responsible? This is the kind of love that cripples rather than empowers.

Toy Storage

The best toy storage does the following:

◆ It fits into your décor.

◆ It's accessible and easy to use.

◆ It doesn't break the family bank.

◆ It's versatile and it has an element of fun!

Look at your toy selection. Remember how I asked you to put everything you have into categories? Your toy storage is dictated by the age of your kids, the amount of space you have, and what toys you have to store.

It's wonderful if your family room offers built-in cupboards. You can have various types of toys on different shelves. It's also nice if your collections are hidden from public view. This way, the room reveals what treasures it holds at your discretion. If you have some wall space, you can get storage units that offer cubbyholes or even have deep shelves built in to serve the same purpose. You could also consider a large basket with a top or a toy chest that closes. Be sure the latter has a hinge that keeps the lid open when the kids are playing so that little fingers don't get smashed. I learned this one the hard way when I was a young child! These types of choices will also allow you to use different spaces for different types of toys.

> **Timely Tidbits**
>
> Help children who haven't yet learned to read by showing a picture of the type of toy to be put into a particular container or drawer. You can have some fun and use a photo of the child holding one of his treasures.

How Crafty of You, My Dear

In Chapter 7, on bedrooms, I mention rolling storage containers as a possibility for children's rooms. In a room that gets outside visitors, you might want something more attractive, such as wicker baskets. In Chapter 8, on closets, I mention plastic, multidrawer units on wheels that give you an instant extra dresser. I mention them again in Chapter 9, on bathrooms, because they're great in bathrooms with extremely limited storage. Well, guess what? They're great for craft supplies, too!

> **Timely Tidbits**
>
> Eliminate and create categories before you head to your local store for your organizing supplies. You have to know what you need to store and where the container will be placed. Stay away from wild colors and unique patterns because they may not be available if you need more containers.

If you have a hobby, remember to peruse the many websites and catalogues devoted to it. I'm sure you will find storage items specifically made for the supplies you need. Finally, never underestimate the power of a few sturdy shelves and some bins for solving your craft problems.

Family Night: Keeping Those Board Games Handy

When it comes to board games, some are timeless and we all know them. I rarely enter a home that doesn't have Monopoly, checkers, chess, or Trivial Pursuit, even if the kids are grown and have their own families. Here are some tricks to make board games easier to access:

♦ Instead of stacking the games flat so that you may have to lift several boxes to get to one on the bottom of the stack, stand them on their sides. Now you can pull several out with ease and the others will still be standing at attention. Be sure they are all facing the same direction so you can read them at a glance.

♦ When it comes to stacking game boxes, don't forget you can use a bookend to keep your stack upright.

♦ If there are lots of parts to a game and little hands are using it daily, as the box ages, you may be afraid you'll lose some parts. Put the loose pieces in plastic bags and return those to the box at the end of a play session.

Timely Tidbits

Craft stores sell plastic bags in many sizes. You won't have to use a big bag from your kitchen; you can get ones that are perfect for what you have to store for each game.

♦ Please note that over time your game boxes may start to deteriorate. You may not be able to store them on their sides without a rubber band around the box.

Piles of Paper

If you need to or choose to pay bills or do other paperwork in this room, don't leave the papers out when you are done for the day. Little sticky fingers can do damage just out of curiosity. Read Chapter 10, on home offices, to learn how to set up a file system. Perhaps you just need one category in this room. For example, you might want to pay bills while you watch TV. Get a portable file box that will look decorative in the room when it's not in use. You can find them in everything from fine leather to wicker. Choose what works best with this room and your budget.

Aftermath

An organized, clutter-free family room that's easy to pick up in seconds will make everyone in the home happier to spend time there. Since the family room is usually used in the evening, it can be pretty messy and lived-in by bedtime. Decide whether you want everyone to pick up before they retire for the evening or first thing in the morning.

This room is ripe with chore possibilities even for the youngest members of the family. You can also designate certain areas as zones to be maintained by specific members of the family only. For example, if Dad cherishes his collection of original Beatles records, he should be the only one to touch them. These kinds of decisions again make for creative solutions that are unique to each family.

The Least You Need to Know

♦ This is a room for collections: records, board games, toys, books, music and video selections, and so on. Each needs to be pared regularly; otherwise, they'll overwhelm the room.

♦ A good system and family teamwork will keep this room in guest-ready condition at all times. Develop a daily 10-minute tidying routine.

♦ If you want to work on projects like scrapbooks, photo albums, or craft projects, be sure the room accommodates all the parts necessary to achieve success.

Chapter 7

Bedrooms: Are They a Sanctuary or a Prison?

In This Chapter

- ◆ How to decide if you have too much furniture
- ◆ How to give new life to furniture you just can't part with
- ◆ How to make your bed in seconds
- ◆ How to make your guests feel welcome and your children secure

I want to tell you a secret. Every single time I go into my bedroom, I smile and say to myself, "I love this room!" It wasn't always so, mind you. If you're reading this book in sequence, you know that I recently did a rather creative makeover of my dining room/living room area. While I was at it, I went crazy and created the bedroom I have always wanted.

I had the walls painted a deep terra cotta. The wall behind my bed has a special effect with a pattern added in gold paint. My painter wasn't sure this was going to work. Now he has it photographed in his portfolio. There is one dresser instead of two;

one straight-back chair (the antique rocker moved to the living room), two bedside tables, and my altar complete the room. The space is functional, personal, yet open and airy. It's my private sanctuary, just as yours should be!

When you walk into your home, you enter the space you have created as your refuge from the world. Ever since 9/11, we have seen an explosion of home shows on TV. We're nesting more. We can't escape totally, can we? Phones, TVs, computers, problems with kids, in-laws, our spouses, our bosses—the list of potential harmony-destroyers is endless. The bedroom, therefore, becomes the sanctuary within the home where we escape from the issues that are part of everyday life. What do you have, a sanctuary or a prison? Let's get to work and create your sanctuary—and if it's already in place, let's kick it up a notch.

Assessment: What's Here and What Tools Do I Need?

Grab your trusty *Declutter Notebook* and a pen, and have a seat in this room. Take a look around. How do you feel when you do this? Is the visual relaxing? Or do you feel stressed, guilty, and anxious? Here are some of the common bedroom clutter offenders I see. Check off the ones you have.

- ❏ The bed is never made. It always looks like you just got up.

- ❏ The closet isn't organized, so clothing rarely makes it to a hanger. Instead, it decorates the chair(s) and the floor.

- ❏ Shoes are kicked off, and pairs are separated and scattered about the room. Some you haven't seen in months.

- ❏ There is a stack of magazines and books so high by the bed that you consider taking up pole-vaulting in the Olympics. After all, you practice at home every night when it's time to get into bed.

- ❏ Your home office is in this room, and piles of papers are scattered everywhere. Sometimes you get up and work at 2 or 3 A.M. when you can't sleep.

- ❏ The kids and the dog are in and out at will, so toys are scattered everywhere.

❏ You have items you don't know what to do with, so they get stashed under the bed. The last time you looked, the Halloween decorations were stored there, along with your wedding album.

❏ There's a TV in this room, and the piles of VHS tapes and DVDs are growing like a fungus in a laboratory.

How did you do? How many did you check off? Was it most or all of them? Take heart. You're in the majority. Here's a big question for you. It may be difficult, so prepare yourself. Do you have too much furniture in this room? It usually has one of two common sources: you moved to this space from a larger one and couldn't part with everything you had, or you inherited some items and the emotional tie is too great to see them move on.

Now we're going to look at the antidotes to all this clutter. As always, your stash of trusty heavy-duty garbage bags is a must.

The Quick Fix

Okay, the first thing you're going to do is to look around and grab any items that you know belong elsewhere in the home. Take a minute to return these things now. For example, is your half-full coffee mug by the bed? Do you have drinking glasses scattered all over the room? Any dishes here from midnight snacks? Let's round up all the kitchen paraphernalia and return it to the kitchen.

Round up your kids' toys, clothing, and other items, and return them to the kids' rooms.

Speaking of items that go elsewhere, do you have too many knick-knacks out? Even valuable antiques can be too many in number to appreciate. Can you move some items to other rooms in the house? Or is it time to pack some away? Rotating decorative items with the seasons isn't just for your dining room display. Do you want to have a new closet system installed but come up short on the cash end? Perhaps some of your treasures could be sold to finance this new era in your life. It's food for thought.

Now I want you to gather up any trash you see. Empty the trash basket, if you have one. All debris gets tossed into the bag.

Hang up the clothes on the chair and put the ones on the floor in your hamper. Don't have one? Let's start a shopping list for this room. You can get a simple one for inside the closet or a fancy one to live in the room, or put a laundry bag on the back of your closet door.

If room in the closet is the issue, you will find all the solutions you need in Chapter 8. If you have to squeeze your clothing in now, take a look and see how many empty wire hangers you have and how many plastic bags from the cleaners are here. Remove those and immediately reclaim a few inches of valuable real estate.

Put your shoes on the closet floor for now. We need to clear the bedroom of debris so we can see what situation we really have here.

Return those VHS tapes and DVDs to the family room. Are there papers that need to go to your office proper or office work area? You know what to do.

If you work in the bedroom, make tidy stacks of the papers. Chapter 10, on the office, includes material on dealing with paper, but as you create your stacks here, don't get lost in them at this time. Feel free to toss anything that you know is no longer needed, like old newspapers, expired coupons, or invitations to events long past.

Why the Bed Has to Be Made

The minute you walk into a room with an unmade bed, you feel sleepy or tired. And, let's face it, it looks sloppy. If "making the bed" to you means taking everything off the bed and making military corners, try rethinking the process. If you tuck your top sheet tightly into the lower part of the bed and sides, you can probably get away with just pulling it up and smoothing it out in the morning. How does that sound?

Timely Tidbits

Would you like to turn your bedroom into a clutter-free, welcoming refuge? Be sure to make your bed every day!

A bedspread usually has to be removed. How about a comforter instead? They are so easy to fluff and put into place. I have a client who hates using a top sheet. She and her husband use only the comforter. They wash the comforter cover each week with the fitted sheet. It takes seconds to make their bed. See how creative you can be. Perhaps you have not been making the bed because you were making it too big a task and thus avoiding it. Let's streamline as we declutter.

Who Really Lives Here?

Let me ask you something about your furniture. If you share your life with someone, did you both agree on everything you see here? I once had a client whose fiancé moved into her condo with only a suitcase. She, on the other hand, was living with all the possessions of her late mother and grandmother. In fact, this had been her mother's condo before her sudden death. When you live with someone you love, your environment needs to express who you are as a couple. There was no room in her condo for that kind of physical or artistic expression. It was crowded when her fiancé moved in.

♦ Is anything crowding your space?

♦ How does your partner feel in this room?

♦ Do you hear some complaints?

♦ How can you make this situation better?

Timely Tidbits

Did your spouse or significant other move into your space? Be sure the décor in the room is balanced. To a man in a frilly, girlie world of ruffles and pink, or a woman forced to live with black and chrome, the bedroom isn't very inviting.

Nightstands

A stack of books and magazines isn't very inviting when piled high on a nightstand. These stacks will probably make you feel guilty long before they invite you to enjoy the treasures they hold. Take a look around the room and see if a small bookcase will fit into the décor. You can keep your current books here and just grab one each night. Magazines go well in magazine holders. We'll talk in detail about books and magazines in Chapter 10. Do you need to add any of these items to your shopping list?

What do you really need by your bedside? The basic items include these:

- A phone
- A notepad
- A pen or pencil
- A good reading light
- A clock
- A small flashlight for emergencies
- Hand cream
- Reading glasses
- Medication, if you need to keep it nearby
- A small bottle of water, especially if you said "yes" to medication

After that, it really depends on you as an individual. What matters is this: is something needed, or is it clutter? Once you make that distinction, you can keep your drawers tidy. Consider lining the drawers; if you need them, use some drawer organizers. You can use whatever you did in the kitchen, or you can get a different design for your liner and perhaps use a different material, like wooden containers (instead of acrylic, plastic, or mesh), here.

That's Entertainment

Personally, I prefer to keep electronic entertainment items out of the bedroom. I see this room as a place to relax and have fun. If you are used to a TV here, perhaps you can keep it in a cabinet or behind a screen. In Chapter 6, we covered several ways to house DVD, VHS, and CD collections in the family room. Try to keep a limited selection here, and choose the holder that works best with your needs and your décor.

When Kids and Pets Take Over the Master Bedroom

While it's certainly wonderful to make our children and pets feel welcome in our private sanctuary, it doesn't have to be a satellite room for them. If you do want to have a few things here, be sure you have a container for them. A nice basket for toys would be great. Do you have one? Add that to your shopping list for this room. By the way, I'm not thinking of a basket the size of a bathtub. Less is more! If your children are young, tell them the items they keep here have to be special. If they walk in with other things, they must leave with them. This is a life skill that will serve them well: return things to their proper location.

What's Under the Bed?

In the best of all possible worlds, the area under the bed remains free space. We cover this in Chapter 8. Remember, if you absolutely need to use this area for storage, be sure the containers you use are designed for this purpose. I am not a fan of cardboard boxes. They fall apart over time, and bugs love to have them for supper. Depending on the height of your bed and the space available, you may want to invest in some containers. They are fairly flat and may be on rollers for easy access. Do you need to check these out at your local home store? Make a note on your shopping list.

This is a good time to assess what is under the bed. Here you want to keep more "benign items" rather than "odd items" like holiday decorations or emotionally charged things like your wedding album. How about out-of-season clothing? Or extra bedding flattened into a nice space bag?

Perilous Pitfalls

Containers for under the bed should be used only if you desperately need the space for storage. Try to avoid cardboard—it falls apart and can turn into a buffet for bugs!

Dresser Drawers: Size and Color Matter

In Chapter 8, on closets, you'll find some basic organizing info for your dresser. The bottom line, as always, is to eliminate all the things you don't (or shouldn't!) be wearing anymore. Here that list includes underwear whose elastic is a memory, bras that couldn't hold up walnuts, and socks that are beyond darning. As soon as these items leave, the dresser usually is pretty roomy.

When you study your room, do you find that you have the right size dresser? Are you sharing it with someone? Do you each need your own? Would a small specialty dresser, such as a lingerie dresser (tall and skinny with multiple drawers), help out by making more room for the man of the house?

If you are tired of your dresser but can't afford to purchase new or additional furniture right now, try these tricks: paint your dresser a festive color and/or get a multiple-drawer unit in plastic from a place like The Container Store to put in your closet. You might also see if you have some items in drawers (sweats and tees, for example) that can now be hung in your newly cleaned closet. There are always ways to work around the ideal solution.

When Your Office Invades Your Bedroom

An office in the bedroom is not the best choice, because it makes it more difficult to get away from your work obligations. If you can, put a screen in front of the area so when you aren't actually working, you won't be able to see your business setup. Try to shut down your computer at day's end so that you won't be tempted to get up in the middle of the night and work. It is important to keep this area tidy.

In a small area, it's critical not only to have a system to handle incoming paper, but also to keep paper that is no longer needed moving out. This may be the "circular file." It should also entail understanding how to set up archival files.

In the meantime, let's take a look at this area and be sure we have indeed cleared away any debris that does not belong here. For instance, do you have equipment you do not use? Many people upgrade to flat-screen monitors without getting rid of those older monitors—you know, the ones that take up the space of a battleship on your desk! A call to your local charity, house of worship, or school will surely put you in touch with someone who would find that monitor (or computer, scanner, printer) a blessing. You can also contact www.sharetechnology.org, an organization that will help you get connected to the place that most needs your electronics.

It seems like everyone is bothered by the ganglia of wires that cascade to the floor from all our equipment. You can try those long plastic tube covers that will wrap around several wires at a time. They come in black or white. Perhaps in today's world, the ideal solution is to go with a wireless setup as much as you can. Try to position your computer so that the wires are flowing to the floor, away from the eyes of all who enter.

Finally, a couple closing questions. Do you have a comfortable chair to sit in? This is always important, but especially so if you spend long hours at this desk. If you are surrounded by supplies, can you put in a small bookcase to hold them, or can you move them to a nearby closet? Keep supplies that you use regularly nearby; back-up supplies are essential, but they needn't be within arm's reach.

Kid's Room: Foundation for His or Her Future Home

If you have young children, be sure to teach them the principles of getting organized from the very beginning. Give them the gift of a clutter-free room and show them not only how to create it, but how to maintain it as well. Teach them with your words and show them with your example. This room really is a microcosm for all the environments they will set up in their lifetimes. Let's make it a good start.

I always have two concerns with a child's room. First of all, are there too many toys? I had a client whose child knew that every time he got a new toy, he had to give one away to a poor child. Most of my clients clean out their children's rooms with them once a year (traditionally, just before school starts) to see what they'd like to donate. With very young children, you can do it for them, with one huge caveat: *Don't let them see you.* No matter how you choose to do it, be sure the room gets a periodic clean sweep.

> **Timely Tidbits**
> Children can help with the decluttering of their rooms by choosing what toys and clothes they're ready to give away. This not only frees up space, but it introduces children to the joy of helping others.

Timely Tidbits _____

Never underestimate the power of paint to add new life to old furniture. If your children are inheriting their furniture, let them put their unique stamp on it with paint, stencils, or stickers.

Does your child have too much furniture? If you are recycling furniture from one child to another, like hand-me-down clothing, perhaps a little paint will make the furniture appear different and allow the child who is inheriting the piece to feel a sense of ownership. Does your child have too much clothing? Excess isn't a way of expressing our love. Dare I say it again? *Less is more!*

Play Today, Then Store Away

There are so many wonderful ways to store toys these days. If you are an Internet person, you can go directly to www.thecontainerstore.com and peruse the world of products available. As I have said, I love storage containers on wheels. They come in three sizes and have lids. It helps children pick up their rooms if they are taught "like goes with like." Barbie has one container, G.I. Joe another; stuffed animals might live on the bed or in a soft toy hammock above the bed. You may prefer large baskets to plastic containers. I had an old-fashioned toy chest when I was growing up. The type of storage isn't key. What matters is learning how to keep related items together.

Timely Tidbits _____

Toy storage containers on wheels are easy for children to move around their rooms. The container can literally go to the scattered toys in question and then return to its designated spot full of the spoils of play.

Every child's room needs a bookcase. If space is at a premium, I hope you will consider putting up at least a shelf or two for books. What goes with a good book—what else but a nice comfy chair for Mom or Dad to sit in while they read to their child? Don't forget a good light source. Just as clothing on the floor or on furniture is a no-no in your room, a child needs to hang up his clothes and have a hamper. Don't let the chair (or the floor!) become a catch-all.

Homework Habitat

One day I was visiting some clients whose young son did his homework at the kitchen table. His parents and I were having a spirited discussion about some topical news. Even Einstein couldn't have maintained his concentration in this small room with three people arguing politics. Suddenly, their son looked up and made a contribution to the conversation—and was reprimanded for not doing his homework!

I have some questions for you: Does your child have a set place to do his homework? Is it well-lit and quiet? Does he have on hand all the supplies he needs? This kind of consistency will help him do his best. We have been decluttering your environment in order to help you succeed in your life. With this simple setup, you can be doing the same with your child.

Many parents feel that homework should be done outside the child's bedroom so that he associates his room with rest. Others feel a bedroom affords the child a chance to work with some privacy. Either way, be sure there are no technological distractions—or, to be more realistic, that they are not being enjoyed during homework time.

Those Terrible Teens

If you feel your teen should be acting in a more grown-up, responsible way with regard to upkeep of his room, ask yourself if the clutter is there because the furniture in the room doesn't support his age level. Is it time, for example, to remove some of those toy containers? Does he need a better/bigger desk with an office chair? As his clothes have gotten bigger, have his closet system and dresser size kept pace?

Is the state of your child's room part of a temporary rebellion, or has he or she never been organized? If it's the former, many parents choose to close the door on the problem with one caveat: no food is to be left in the room. Very often a session with a professional organizer or an organized and trusted family friend can bring the teen around. Kids always tell me they are living with a mess because they know it drives their parents up the wall. I suggest they get organized to support their own lives and find another way to rebel.

If your child has never been organized, what is the cause? If you have not been a role model up to this point, perhaps after using this book you can show your child your organized bedroom and ask if they would like some help creating the same clutter-free and organized environment for themselves. If you have another issue at play, like ADD or ADHD, you may want to consult a book, therapist, or educator geared toward dealing with those specific issues.

The Case of the Messy Stepson

At this point, I feel you need a story. A friend of mine had the "messiest stepson in the world." His room was an active tornado at all times. She would give up and tell him not only "No food in your room," but also "No mess outside your room." One day she called in tears over the stinky gym socks and sneakers he was perpetually leaving in the living room. Mind you, this is one of the most organized women on the planet. His behavior nearly drove her mad.

All of his life, her stepson had been taught how to clean, do laundry, shop, sew, and so on. When he went off to college, she assumed he'd be living like a pig. Guess what? At college, he was the one who not only couldn't stand a mess, but couldn't deal with his housemates' clutter. They had never been taught how to clean, cook, or do laundry! He started being the go-to guy in his dorm. It may seem your words are falling on deaf ears, but trust me: your child is getting the message.

Guest Room: Is the Welcome Mat Out?

I once stayed in a guest room that was so uninviting, I literally cried myself to sleep. The small room was filled with a huge bed. There were no hangers for my clothes, no space in the closet, and absolutely no amenities in the room. I couldn't sneak off by myself and read a book, watch a little TV, or listen to a radio. The room felt oddly like a prison—albeit, one with designer bedding!

If you're lucky enough to have a dedicated guest room, take a look around and see how the current setup would make you feel if you came for a visit. If you are using this room as a storage closet, make some decisions about the items that have been dumped here. Then you can enjoy this room and have company over more often.

Very few people have dedicated guest rooms. Those lucky enough to have an extra room make sure it serves multiple purposes. It's very often a makeshift gym and/or an office most of the year. Here is where you need to ask yourself a question: How often do I need this room as a guest room? I had a client who had her mother over for two weeks a year. The room was to be an office the other 50 weeks of the year. But it didn't work well as an office. When she asked me why, I figured out the problem the minute the door opened. My client had a queen-size bed smack in the middle of the room. It ate up almost all the floor space and made it nearly impossible to get to the desk and office supplies.

Do you relate to this scenario? Take a look at your guest bed. If it's a large bed eating up a vast amount of floor space, it's clutter. It may be time for it to go. Get a day bed. Get a futon couch that opens up. Where's that shopping list? We may need to add to it now!

Remember how we talked about the importance of categories? Place your office paraphernalia in one part of the room and your gym equipment or craft supplies in another. If you have hardwood floors, you're in luck. You can use inexpensive area rugs to visually demarcate the uses in the room.

Make an honest assessment of your workout equipment. Does anyone in the home use the exercise equipment regularly? Or are you a weekend warrior who uses the space sporadically? If you are the latter, perhaps it's time to sell the bulk of the equipment and use those funds to purchase one machine that works the whole body. Or perhaps you have space in the garage you could convert to a gym area. This works well if you live in a temperate climate where the car can be on the street or in the driveway in all seasons.

> **Perilous Pitfalls**
>
> No matter where you decide to work out, be sure you have a full-length mirror. You want to check your posture and your form in order to avoid injury. Proper flooring is also a must, to help absorb shocks and/or provide a non-slip surface.

The Empty Nest

Raising children is a sacred task. It is difficult, expensive, time-consuming, exhausting—and the most important and rewarding work on the planet. Inherent in the silent covenant between parent and child at birth is the promise that one day the child will leave the home, perhaps start his own family, and surely share his gifts with the world. Nowhere in this arrangement is the idea that his room will be turned into a museum. It happens, though, doesn't it?

If your children are in college, surely it is a comfort for them to be able to return home to familiar quarters on weekends or holidays. Once they're on their own, though, you need to determine the function of this room. Practically speaking, do you need it as a guest room, craft room, gym, or home office? If it can remain dedicated to your child when he returns for a visit, could you pack away items like stuffed animals and sports trophies?

Ask your children to decide what they want to take to their adult homes once they are established, and donate the rest to the charity of your choice. Don't allow yourself to become the free off-site storage your children depend on. Set a timetable for distribution of these items.

School Papers and Artwork: Save Only the Gems

My mother was a typical mother of an only child. She saved everything I touched for the first eight years of school. Notebooks? Check. Papers? Check. Artwork? Check. I actually didn't realize this collection existed until a few years after she and my father had died. The night before the movers came, I discovered this secret stash of memorabilia.

Parents, take note: I was not grateful. I was burdened by my mother's inability to make a decision about what I might want as an adult. I can't speak for everyone, of course, but the bottom line for me was this: very little was needed or wanted. I made decisions that night for eight years of my life—decisions my mother should have made, or better yet, made with me. And I did it in minutes. The moral is this: do your children a favor and save only the gems.

In any art supply store, you will find large, acid-free paper art portfolios. Put the best artwork from the year here. Ask your child to help you pick what should stay. Get a portfolio for each child and label it with their name and the year. As for school papers, decide why you would want a particular paper. Save the best, the extraordinary, or the touching, not everything they turn in. There are beautiful, archival-quality storage boxes that can easily hold the small treasures of a particular school year. One per child again, labeled with the child's name and the year.

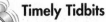

Timely Tidbits

Teach your children to be creative with the way they save items they want to include in their personal memorabilia. A photo of them wearing a favorite outfit takes up a lot less space in an album than the actual outfit does hanging for years in their closet.

Baby Clothes and Toys: Pack 'Em Up, Move 'Em Out

I have learned over the years that mothers are very attached to baby clothes, especially if they're having only one child or when they get to what they know will be the last baby. In *The Zen of Organizing*, my first book, I describe a phenomenon I call "the magic talisman." I have found we place great significance on a particular object from a time in our lives that we treasure. We think it will magically restore that time to us if we have this clothing, furniture, or knick-knacks near us. Having Grandma's rocking chair in the living room can indeed give us a sense of continuity.

We can't, however, have all of Grandma's furniture unless we live in a huge house and share exactly the same taste in possessions. Even then, we would be denying ourselves the chance to find our own treasures in life—or, better yet, the treasures that express our relationship with our partner. It's the same with clothing.

Timely Tidbits

Resist the temptation to turn your grown child's room into a shrine. Keep the best of the artwork, a special toy like a first teddy bear, and perhaps one baby outfit. Toss or donate the rest.

Save one or two outfits, perhaps with an eye to your grandchildren enjoying them. Give the rest to a charity, especially one that caters to sick or dying children whose parents may not be able to afford such treasures. In this way, rather than being a relic, the item is allowed to do good in the world. No matter how long you save these baby clothes, your child will not be wearing them again.

As I write this, I have my first teddy bear sitting in my living room. He is a very small guy and very dear to me. He's the only treasure I have from my childhood and the only one I need. Toys are like clothes: they need to keep moving or find their final resting place somewhere else. Dragging large numbers of them with you and having them litter your current environment with the past serves no one.

Aftermath

Keeping your bedroom clutter-free takes daily diligence. Your clothes go back into the closet at day's end, for example, not onto the floor or the back of a chair. This might be a great new habit for you to consciously practice for 21 (consecutive) days.

Be aware of books and magazines creeping back onto the nightstand. Remember, these are meant to bring you pleasure, not add pressure to your life. Bring them to your bedside table one at a time from your (new) bookcase and savor them.

You'll have to sell the new rules about toys to your children, not as a punishment, but as a way to make the use of this room special to them. Show them that this behavior is exactly how Mom and Dad make their bedroom special.

> **Perilous Pitfalls**
>
> Practice daily hanging up your clothes, putting away magazines and books, and limiting your kid's clutter in your space. Keep it up, or your clutter will return to taunt you.

Not every change here will be immediate. Yes, the physical landscape will be clutter-free, but it may take some time until you're able to divest yourself of that extra furniture. Take heart. When the time is right, it will happen. If at first you don't succeed ....

The Least You Need to Know

♦ The bed has to be made every day.

♦ Clothing has to be returned to the closet or placed in the hamper or the dry cleaners bag.

♦ This room is the last room you see at night and the first you see in the morning. Having it clutter-free will bookend your day in peace and calm.

Chapter 8

Closets: Can You Find Anything to Wear?

In This Chapter

- Learn how professional organizers set up closets
- Find space you didn't know you had at your disposal
- Learn the tricks of the trade for your clothes closet
- Protect your off-season clothing and delicates like cashmere sweaters
- Get your shoes under control at last
- Streamline your linen closet

I have to assume that every professional organizer has his or her favorite part of the home to organize. My favorite is the closet. Not just your clothes closet, mind you, but all the closets in the home. I find them fascinating. As we unearth your "stuff," inevitably within the clutter, the story of your life reveals itself.

The interesting thing about clothes closets is that they are rarely put together with any rhyme or reason. This is interesting because we all shop in stores. Whether it's your local department store or a high-end boutique on Rodeo Drive in Beverly Hills, the same basic setup rules apply. For some reason, we're looking at the patterns but not duplicating them at home. As you make your way through this chapter, you will learn all the tricks of the trade.

Assessment: What's Here and What Tools Do I Need?

It's time to take out your *Declutter Notebook* and write down all the complaints you have about your clothes closet, probably the most important closet in your home. Let's see how many I can guess:

◆ I can never find what I want.

◆ There are too many sizes here.

◆ I love shoes. I can't stop buying them.

◆ There's no room for storage.

◆ I have no idea how to handle my seasonal items.

What would you add to this list?

Tools to the Rescue

When it comes to tools, one thing you need is one style of hanger. Wood is my favorite; it protects your clothes like nothing else. In some closets, however, wood eats up too much of the space. The thin plastic hangers with the open space for spaghetti-strap garments are perfect. These are fragile, so you need to handle with care. Tubular hangers are also fun and acceptable. Use only one color. If you are sharing the space, each of you can adopt a color.

You can't purchase your new hangers at this stage, however. We need to see how much we can eliminate first. After that, you'll be able to take an accurate count.

No matter what hanger you choose, remove all the wire hangers your cleaner has sent home with you over the years. These will destroy shape and fabric over time. And your friendly neighborhood cleaner will no doubt be delighted when you return the wire ones. Practical recycling at its best!

Perilous Pitfalls

Wire hangers can ruin the shape of your garments. In addition, the average cleaner uses chemicals that may be carcinogenic. Keeping plastic covers in place seals in those chemicals until you wear the garment again. Toss the hangers and the plastic the minute you get home.

Those famous heavy-duty garbage bags will be a godsend for transporting clothing and other miscellaneous closet items to the trash, to charity, or wherever. Keep your *Declutter Notebook* handy so you can create your shopping/wish list of closet products.

I recommend a two-step step stool in your closet if you have high shelves, or if you are short and the clothing bars were set high when they were installed. I remember one closet in a New York apartment that looked like it had been set up for giants. I'm 5'9" and could barely reach the bars. If you don't feel you need a step stool here permanently, store it in the kitchen or laundry area. A small stool with no back folds up flat and is easy to store. This is a must-have for every home—unless, of course, you play professional basketball and can reach those high places with ease.

The Quick Fix

In this chapter, our quick fixes happen in stages. The first wave helps us deal with all the hanging clothes. When I organize a closet, I do two things immediately: I remove all the wire hangers and plastic bags from the cleaners. You have no idea what space-takers these items are until you see the results. If you do have clothing (summer whites, evening clothes, and so on) that needs to be covered, invest in canvas covers from The Container Store. Canvas allows your clothes to breathe and won't stain them as plastic may over time. It's also healthier; plastic bags can seal in cleaning agents that may be carcinogenic.

Hang 'Em High

Promise me you won't put all of your hanging clothes on your bed. I hear some professional organizers suggest this. The idea is that only what you want to keep goes back into the closet. Good luck. It will be so wrinkled, you'll have to iron it or send it to the cleaners. Let's not go there.

Timely Tidbits

If you store suitcases in your closet, don't put the smaller ones inside the larger. Your small bags may have been in planes, trains, automobiles, and other places where they can pick up dirt. This dirt will now be deposited in your big suitcase, only to decorate your clothes.

If your closet is so jammed with clothing that you can't maneuver, try using a portable clothing rack. These aren't expensive, and they fold flat for easy storage. Perhaps a friend already has one you can borrow. If you travel frequently, these portable racks will help you by being the place you pull out your travel wardrobe.

Other Closets—Share the Wealth

If you have closets in your home that aren't being used, you may want to move some categories of clothing to them now to permanently free up space in your main clothes closet. Evening clothes are one example. Perhaps you ski or engage in another seasonal sport that requires a specific wardrobe? Hang these clothes in a guest room closet, if you have one, or pack them away until you need them. If your closet is small but the room is fairly large, invest in something like an armoire so you have instant additional hanging and drawer space.

New Homes for Miscellaneous Items

The next step is to pull out anything from your closet that is not related to clothing. The most common items I find are these: free weights, portable fans, a box or two of memorabilia or loose photos in search of an album, and guns. Yes, I said guns. For some reason, this is where a family often hides a gun and ammo. The most outlandish item I ever found, by the way, was the ashes of my client's first wife. Ideally, all these items need to find a new home.

Let's take a look at your miscellaneous items before we move on. Try to find a more appropriate home for everything unrelated to clothing. I fully realize this may not be possible if you live in a tiny apartment and have no extra storage. We're going for the best of all possible worlds here, and you can tailor my ideas to suit your unique situation. If non-clothing items need to stay, we're on a quest to store them the best way we can.

A visual cacophony, so to speak, of multicolored or broken-down cardboard boxes will be a disturbing visual every time you open your closet. Keep things simple. Photos, for example, should be in photo storage boxes, not tossed into one or two big cardboard boxes. Instead of feeling guilty every time you open the closet because you haven't gotten around to making some albums, you'll be gently reminded that this project is on your "Project Wish List."

By the way, as you make your albums, think about putting them out to share with family and friends. I frequently see completed albums hidden away. Why not put them on a bookcase in the living room or family room so they are easy to reach? Don't you want to regularly enjoy the fruits of your labors?

Try to put those free weights under the bed. You'll still be able to grab them easily. Of course, a totally free space under the bed is best, but weights are a pretty benign item and I know you want them handy. I recently organized a woman who had saved a box of hate mail from a relative under her bed. Not a good idea to have emotionally upsetting things anywhere in the private sanctuary of your bedroom. If you have one or more guns in the bedroom to protect your family, follow the rules of gun safety, especially if there are children in the home. A locked gun cupboard or safe is ideal.

Perilous Pitfalls

Go to www.ehow.com for advice on gun storage safety (www.ehow.com/how_3849_store-guns-safely.html).

Shelves Optional

If you find that you have nowhere else to store items unrelated to your clothing, try this: look in your closet. Most of them have at least one shelf above the rods. If you look above that shelf, you usually see a huge space between it and the ceiling. Consider installing a new shelf for your orphaned items or, better yet, your off-season clothes.

All it takes is putting wood braces on either side and laying a simple piece of lumber across. I prefer wood to all other types of shelves, for its sturdiness. This is especially important if you need to store heavy items like photos. You might also decide to remove one or two of the shorter rods, if you have a walk-in closet, for example, and build a series of shelves.

Complete One Step at a Time

I would take to other locations all items that can live elsewhere. If you have to purchase photo boxes or other items and need to continue to store your collections here, set everything to one side in your bedroom. We need to organize your closet first, before you will truly know what is available to you in terms of space. Depending on the size of your closet, these items may take you up to a day to deal with properly. Take heart. I am sure they have been migrating here over the years, so waiting one day to deal with them properly is really small in the scheme of things.

Don't Get Hung Up on the Hang-Up

Are you ready to move on to your hanging clothes? Okay, don't look at anything else. The shoes and the shelves will wait.

Set Your Own Closet Rules

People always ask me what the rule is for clothing. Sometimes they tell me they know: it's one new item in, one old one out, or "If you haven't worn it in six months (or a year), toss it." I have no interest in such arbitrary rules, and neither should you.

I ask my clients one simple question about each article of clothing: "Do you wear this?" If the answer is "Yes," the garment stays. If I hear "No," it goes to a charity or someone they designate. There is an entire world that lies between a definitive "Yes" and "No." And that is the world of emotional attachment.

Here are the most common reasons people hold on to clothes they no longer wear. See if you can relate to any of these before we begin selecting clothing you want to keep. Once you understand the emotional power of these attachments, you can make the choice to detach, and then cleaning out your closet will be a breeze.

- ◆ You have a wardrobe of suits from when you were in the working world.

- ◆ You have clothes that are way too small to wear. You hope one day to fit into them again.

- ◆ You have a "fat wardrobe," just in case you gain weight again.

- ◆ You have garments that were expensive, and you're waiting for them to come back into style.

- ◆ You have clothing items that were given to you by someone you love who is no longer here.

- ◆ You have garments from a time in your life that has passed.

If even one of these strikes a chord with you, take heart. You are not alone. Here is what I would tell you if we were working together. I hope this advice helps you view your physical possessions in a new light.

Treasure It or Toss It

First of all, the common ground all these concerns share is a need to hold on to the past—but clothing can't really do that for you. Unless, for example, you plan to return to the workforce in the very near future, your suits are going to get more outdated by the minute and take up valuable space in your closet. Donate them to a charity that helps impoverished women dress for their first job interviews. Save one, if you're really attached. Better yet, see if you have any photos of yourself in these outfits.

If you were once a much smaller size, won't you want to celebrate with some fresh new styles when you return to that size? So maybe save one pair of your smallest jeans as a weight-loss test. Conversely, if you have achieved your goals, why hold on to a larger wardrobe to remind you of bad times?

Neither clothing we have purchased in happier eras nor those garments we have inherited will take us back in time or restore our loved ones to us. I don't advocate the wholesale tossing of sentimental items. I ask that you pick and choose. One of my clients, for example, had saved a dress from her only pregnancy. Her son was almost grown now. He had been a late-in-life baby. I suggested that she take one of the pictures she had of herself wearing the dress when she was pregnant and have it framed in a shadow box or put in a scrapbook along with a swatch of fabric from the dress. This is a lovely way to remember the past without clogging up your closet today.

Fashion Rules

Finally, let me say a word about the cycle of fashion. While it is absolutely true that just about every style returns if you wait long enough, you have to have an enormous house to keep all those clothes! We want to create room in your closet so you can truly see what you have.

Is It Even Wearable?

The simple questions are: Do you wear this? "Yes," and it stays. "No," and you need to ask "Why not?" Before you get into the complicated emotional responses, take a look at the garment. Is it discolored? Frayed? Will you feel good wearing it? Is it the correct size? Very often, practical considerations will cause you to grab your donation bag long before you need to get to any underlying emotion.

One Garment at a Time ... Go!

Remember my warning that the whole of anything is overwhelming? Take just one garment at a time in your hands and work section by section. After you remove all the hanging clothing you no longer want or need, take those bags out of your bedroom immediately. Get them to the charity of your choice the same day—or at least out to the trunk of your car. It's funny how items can magically migrate back to the closet if left in the home. Don't second-guess yourself.

Here are the simple rules for a professionally organized closet:

- ◆ Using one type of hanger, have all clothing face the same direction.

- ◆ Get shoes off the floor.

- ◆ Keep types of clothing grouped together so that blouses and shirts, slacks and jeans, suits, skirts and dresses, and so on are all in individual areas.

Color-Coding

The best way to keep categories of clothing organized is to use color. For me, the following color progression works best: white/off white, beige/brown, blue/purple, pink/red/orange, green/yellow, and gray/black. I use this order in every section of the hanging wardrobe.

I also repeat this same pattern with shoes, purses, stacks of sweaters, and all other clothing groups. I even repeat the pattern in drawers so that my clients always know exactly where to look for anything in their wardrobe. You may want to use another progression. I had a client who started with black. Just be consistent!

Color-Coding as You Fold 'Em

Speaking of repeated patterns, remember how you dealt with your hanging items? You'll be using the same criteria for your shoes, sweaters, and the contents of your drawers.

Each remaining category (shoes, sweaters, scarves, and so on) should first be cleaned out with a quick-fix sweep. My clients start to pick up my lingo. When the hanging clothes are done, they will inevitably pick up a pair of scuffed, worn-down shoes and say: "I know, Regina, it's tired." Off it goes to the charity donation bag or the trash. In the same vein, do you really want to wear sweaters that have shrunk or those with moth holes or underarm stains? They go in those tired piles, too.

Timely Tidbits

It's really important to get your full trash and donation bags out of this room as quickly as possible. This will keep your workspace clear and help you see the positive results of your decluttering efforts.

> **Timely Tidbits** _____
>
> In addition to cedar, you can introduce lavender to your closet for natural protection against moths. Another item to use—tobacco. Ancient rug merchants rolled tobacco in pouches with their rugs. You can make your pouches using canned tobacco and cheesecloth. You can also sprinkle cedar balls in and around your sweater stacks.

Like Items Should Stick Together

When I was growing up in Brooklyn, we were blessed with deep closets. I never saw a walk-in closet until I moved to L.A. Whether you can walk into your closet and create true physical areas or you have one long rod to hang your clothing in sequential groupings, do keep related items together. When all your blouses, jeans, and suits and other clothes live in separate areas, you will always be able to find what you are looking for. And that equates to time saved.

Closet Doors

Now let's talk closet doors. They aren't created equal. If you have sliding doors, I extend my sympathy. Aren't they the biggest pain in the neck ever? Place your clothing categories in the order in which you reach for them. This way you won't be opening and closing those doors as frequently. If you own your home, think about installing regular doors. If you rent, ask if the doors could be stored. You can put up an inexpensive shade.

> **Perilous Pitfalls** _____
>
> Clutter collects when you don't want to be bothered sliding closet doors back and forth. Where do the clothes go? The usual suspects are the back of a chair or, worse, the floor.

Footwear Fun

Let's look at your shoes. If you're a guy, you probably don't have that many. If you're gal, you may have enough to make Imelda Marcos green with envy. Let's consider the best ways to store shoes, and then you can choose what works best for your personal collection. The one rule of thumb is this: get them off the floor! Here are the best choices.

Shoe Racks

If you're a woman who wears lots of heels, an expandable metal shoe rack will work well for you. You can also stack these shoe racks if you have a lot of shoes and the necessary vertical space. The trick here is that the thin bar of the shoe rack holds the shoe in place if there is a heel. Flats, summer sandals, and exercise shoes will slide onto the floor.

Shoe Bags

If you have a solid door on your closet (if not, what about the back of the bedroom door?), you can hang a canvas shoe bag. I prefer canvas to the metal variety. This is an excellent solution for your sports shoes. Canvas doesn't clang against the door every time it's opened or closed. As a fabric, it also gives and accommodates a bigger shoe with ease.

The Wonders of Wood

A great shoe rack that is made for men's shoes but works just as well for women's flats and exercise shoes is a stacking shoe rack made out of wood. If you find it in cedar, you'll be adding a touch of moth protection to your closet. In addition, you can find a wood shoe holder that has cubicles for your shoes. It doesn't expand, but it's usually made to hold several pairs of shoes; it might just fit the bill for your closet space and shoe needs.

Clear Shoeboxes

Ladies, we all seem to have one or two pairs of evening shoes that we don't wear that often. Instead of keeping them in the box from the store, I'd like to introduce my all-time favorite shoe-storage solution. It's a clear shoebox with a pull-out tray. You can stack them up to the ceiling and still be able to get your shoes without moving any of the boxes. I purchase the larger size so that the highest heel will always fit. In fact, you can use this as your only shoe storage.

Cardboard Shoeboxes

Store-bought shoeboxes come in all shapes and sizes. If you're stacking by shoe color, you may wind up with the shoebox version of the leaning tower of Pisa. This is the chief reason keeping the original shoebox is not my favorite shoe-storage solution. If you prefer it, however, attach a photo of the shoe on the outside and keep your stacks short.

These Boots Are Made for Walking and Storing

Of course, no discussion of shoes would be complete without mentioning boots. First of all, I think it's important to put boot shapers in tall boots so that they keep their shape. Guess what? It also makes them easier to store. I do keep boots on the floor of the closet during the winter. As you might guess, they are lined up in color order. Once the warm weather arrives, you may want to store them in special containers. This might be a soft pouch that came with them or the original box, or you can purchase one made for this purpose from The Container Store. Don't forget to treat the leather regularly so they stay supple for years to come.

If you live in snow country, you might want to keep your snow boots or hiking boots in your mudroom, if you have one, or in the hall closet closest to the front door. If you enter through the garage, have a place for shoes to dry—and have house slippers waiting for you.

Storage Solutions

Now that you have your hanging clothes and shoes in order, you are probably feeling pretty good. Pat yourself on the back. That's a huge accomplishment. But it's the remaining items—like purses, sweaters, hats, and gloves—that can cause a problem. And we don't want to destroy the order we've created by having messy shelves. As long as you whittle down your collections to exactly what you know you need and will use, we'll find a way to make them all work. There are wonderful products out there to assist you.

> **Perilous Pitfalls**
>
> Unless you know exactly which organizing products you need and how many, don't purchase products on impulse. They will inevitably become more clutter.

Purses Need Space

I am more of a purse freak than a shoe collector. Big feet are the culprit, I am afraid. I always look for ways to store my small collection of bags. If you have fine leather or suede bags, do keep them in the drawstring bags they traditionally come with. I like my purses in color order, of course, on a shelf. Ladies, if your purses flop over when empty, consider filling them with a bit of tissue paper. They will be easier to store and will keep their shape for years to come. If you have a large collection, you can use a shelf divider to keep them tidy and erect.

Sweaters Need Space, Too

This same handy tool, the shelf divider, will keep sweater stacks from imploding. The number of sweaters you own will guide you to a storage/display solution. I like to see sweaters in color stacks divided by a shelf divider. While it's nice to fold sweaters exactly the way they do in the store, the important thing is that you are consistent.

You may also want to store sweaters in sweater boxes. These are clear so you can see what's inside, and you can pull out the drawer as you did with the shoebox and gain easy access.

These wonderful boxes come in various sizes, so you can also use them for scarves, hats, gloves, and fine-gauge shawls or pashminas. This is a great way to store these items when the season ends. Just move them to a higher shelf in their acrylic boxes or set them in the back of the closet on the floor till next winter.

Clear Hat Boxes—for Hats, Scarves, and Special Stuff

Another way to store small items like lightweight scarves is to put them in a clear, round, acrylic hatbox. I love this item. You can be creative with the contents. For my female clients who have active social lives, I store their evening purses here. The purses are shielded from dust and always on display. Ladies usually have some belts that simply can't be hung. I like to roll those and place them in an acrylic hatbox or a decorative basket. Again, the beauty of storing hats or any other item here is that you can see what you have.

Racking Up Ties and Belts

If you have wall space in your closet, consider a tie and/or a belt rack if you wear those items. Depending on the number, you might even get a wall unit that handles both.

You won't be surprised to learn that I label either all of my containers or the shelf area just in front of them.

Closet Dead—Space, That Is

Some closets have what I call dead pockets. The rod extends the length of the closet, but close to 2 feet extends between the wall of the closet and a wall in the room. What to do? I would use this area for off-season storage. Getting back there will always be a drama. You might also consider having shelves put in. Yes, you'll have clothes in front of your shelves, but you can use this for off-season items.

Closet Furniture for Your Walk-In Closet

If you are blessed with a large walk-in closet, you might want to place a dresser inside. It can be additional to the one in your bedroom, or it can be the only one, thus giving you more room in the bedroom proper. A full-length mirror on the back of the door is always helpful. Don't forget to use a hand mirror for a quick once-over. You want to be sure you're as chic from the sides and the back as the front view suggests.

On top of the dresser, you can have your jewelry boxes. Many of my clients put up corkboard above the dresser and use tacks to hang their long necklaces. There are the traditional wood jewelry boxes as well as acrylic jewelry containers for earrings, necklaces, bracelets, and all manner of jewelry. Of course, these are great for your costume pieces only. When good jewelry isn't on you, it should be locked away.

> **Timely Tidbits**
>
> Light is very important in your closet. It's difficult to distinguish some colors. Portable lights that you can install yourself or a visit from your friendly electrician will be of tremendous help as you get dressed each day.

Declutter de Dresser

No matter where your dresser is, we want it to be clutter-free. Most of the drawers I open are so crammed with stuff that they can barely open. We tend to buy new socks, underwear, bras, and the like without tossing out the old ones.

The Container Store has special containers you can use for bras, panties, men's underwear, and socks that fit right in the drawer. They have all kinds of choices, from wood for men and fabric for ladies, to simple plastic for the kids. Sports socks are so bulky that you might want to put a small container or bin on the floor and toss them inside.

> **Perilous Pitfalls**
>
> If you invest in a home safe, be sure it isn't so lightweight that it can be carried from room to room. Your friendly thief will be so grateful that you boxed up everything for him.

Outta the Drawers—into the Drawers

By the way, you may find you have some items in your dresser that you've now got room to hang (blue jeans come to mind) because you've created space in your closet. Conversely, you may find that you have some empty drawers. Perhaps some of your hanging garments might like to migrate to the dresser? Pjs, tees, and sweats are frequently in this category. Don't be afraid to shake up the existing order.

Silly Jewelry

Ask yourself the same questions about your jewelry that you did with your clothing. Costume jewelry is fun, but it's frequently a whimsical purchase. You don't have to hang on to those Mardi Gras necklaces forever. Nor will you need the banana earrings from the zoo. Ask yourself if you enjoyed them when you wore them and then let them go. Maybe you know some small children who like to play dress-up?

Closet Clutter—Hats and Shirts

Two huge culprits in terms of drawer clutter are vacation baseball caps and T-shirts. Trust me, that Hawaiian shirt is appropriate only in

Honolulu. If you can't part with old T-shirts from vacation stops, put them in a nice container and tuck them into the deepest recesses of your closet (or basement or attic). This way, the nice new tees you have will have space to breathe. I have a friend who travels the world for work. She frequently makes toss pillows for her beach house out of her travel tees.

As for those baseball caps, gentlemen, I know you are attached. How about hanging three or four on a hook in your closet and putting the rest away with those old, albeit treasured, T-shirts? Wanna remember that special trip? Make a photo album. I am sure there is at least one picture of you in your favorite cap. You could even make a Baseball Cap Album! I smell a trend.

Closet Clutter—Paper and Memorabilia

By the way, if you open the top drawer of your dresser and you see a growing stash of slips of paper and receipts, you need to transport these to your office area. We'll deal with these and all manner of paper in Chapter 10. I once had a client who kept receipts in her lingerie drawer. This was at once extremely creative and extremely inappropriate.

In the kitchen, we used small containers to keep the contents of drawers in line. Guess what? We can use those same tools here. In a closet, I'd probably get them in wood. While they are great for small items, if you're a guy, you may want to have something a little fancier. Fortunately, there are special containers made just for you.

Another clutter culprit in the average closet is a box of memorabilia. I find that parents of young children very often have a box of mementos from their preparental days. I would pare this to a respectful minimum. In the best of all possible worlds, tuck a storage box of these items in your basement or attic. Eras we lived through become a part of the very fabric of our lives; they really don't live in "stuff." You carry the best part of the experience with you. It's called your memories.

Closet Systems to the Rescue

If you own your home, you may want a professional closet company to come in and redesign the space and install a new system. This is costly but surely increases the value of your home. These systems are all made of wood or melamine. Be sure to ask your closet designer for the following:

Perilous Pitfalls

If you inherited a closet system, be sure it is properly reinforced. I have had closet systems at the swankiest addresses you can imagine come crashing to the floor under the weight of an average wardrobe. Your clothes can get wrinkled or soiled, and you can be hurt.

- ◆ Have holes drilled all the way down each panel. This way, you have the option later of either moving the rod(s) to different heights or removing them altogether and ordering shelves.

- ◆ If you have a very tall person in the home, be sure you use an article of clothing like a dress shirt when you are measuring. If a man is well over 6 feet, for example, a particular area may not accommodate two bars. You want those shirts to have ample space to hang and not be dragging on the floor or knocking into the next rod.

- ◆ Ask for one or two pull-out rods. They pull out and help you plan an outfit, and then tuck back into the wall.

- ◆ If you can, have them install a pull-out tray. You'll be able to fold things in the closet.

- ◆ You may also want some of your shelves to have glass doors. This way, you can store items without containers and they will remain dust-free.

- ◆ Finally, be sure all of your shelves, especially the ones for shoe storage, are adjustable. Glass doors on your shoe collection will eliminate the need for any kind of shoe-storage boxes, and your shoes will be dust-free.

If, like me, you're a renter, you might want a less expensive system that will not break your bank but will make life easier. Take a look at the Elfa System in The Container Store. Take the dimensions of your closet with you to the store, and they will space-plan every closet in your home with you for free.

I am a fan of a bed with absolutely nothing stored under it. If you live in tight quarters with ill-designed closets, however, you may need to store your off-season clothing here. There are storage containers that are made to slide under the bed. Some have drawers and wheels so you have easier access to those items. Or you might consider a platform bed that has drawers built in. If you need to use this space, it might as well be convenient.

Less Is More

Clothes closet organizing can be a tough job depending on a host of variables, including how much clothing you have, what kind of closet space, and how attached you are to what you own. Once it's done, however, my slogan "Less is more" will prove true as you get dressed and start your day with ease because everything you own is at your fingertips. Enjoy your clothes. Save time. And always look your best.

Toddlers to Teens: Be Just Like Mom and Dad

The biggest clutter culprit I find in kids' closets is their parents' stuff! Allow your children to own their own space.

One of the first things kids want to do, in order to assert some self-control and appear to be grown-up, is to pick their own clothes to wear. If you have an area in the closet for two rods, you can put dressy, costume, or good-quality clothing on the top rod or bar, where little hands can't reach. On the low bar in the closet, hang everyday clothing choices. Many parents give their children a step stool to help them. I wouldn't introduce this, of course, until their balance is secure.

Put a shoe rack on the floor or a hanging shoe rack on the door. Separate their clothing stacks with shelf dividers just like in your closet. You will make them feel so grown-up! You will also be teaching them the basics. You can find all of these pint-sized and regular products at The Container Store. The Elfa system can be tweaked to fit your child's closet needs as they grow from toddler to teen.

The Elfa system has drawer units that you can use as a dresser for little tees, shorts, tops, and the like. In the child's dresser you can put socks, underwear, pjs, and the like. Try to keep some of these items in the lower drawers so that, once again, your children can begin as soon as possible to dress themselves.

If you need more space for clothes that can be folded but you don't want a closet system, there are some nice plastic storage units on wheels that have multiple drawers. You can tuck them into a corner of the room or into the closet if there is space. As your child grows, they can be used for toy storage, can even help you store craft supplies or photos, or can move to the garage or laundry area. The right tools usually have many applications that make them worth the expense.

Guest-Room Closet

Your guests deserve about 18 inches of hanging space in the closet and some hangers for various types of clothing. It's a nice touch if you can have the same type of hanger. Don't foist your old wire hangers on your guests; this is recycling gone mad.

A little floor space under this area is great. If you have supplied a shoe rack, you get a prize. The trick is to organize the closet so that it doesn't look as if you simply shoved aside assorted debris for a few hangers. The goal is for your guests to feel welcome.

The average guest-room closet is used for many things. Here are some decluttering ideas for the most typical situations:

♦ If you have a lot of out-of-season clothes stored here, you might want to put them in canvas covers. In addition to the individual covers for suits, dresses, and evening wear that I mentioned earlier, you can get extra-wide canvas covers that hold multiple pieces. This is ideal for long-term storage. Your wardrobe will stay clean and protected.

♦ Do you store photos and memorabilia here? Follow the instructions mentioned earlier in this chapter, and put your items in appropriate containers. If you won't have time to make albums for a while, consider archival-quality storage boxes.

Timely Tidbits

Containers designed for one type of storage can be cleverly used for something the designer didn't have in mind. In this way, you get to express your creativity and have some fun. I use clear shoeboxes with lids to store craft supplies.

◆ Long on desire to do craft projects but short on storage space? This is a great closet for that extra shelf I suggested earlier. You can sort your supplies into categories and store them in attractive boxes. These can be placed on the top shelf. You can also use one of the rolling units we considered for a child's room.

Hall Closets

Growing up on the East Coast, I assumed that all homes and apartments had hall closets. It's such a logical place to store your guests' coats in the cold months. It's also the place to keep your heaviest coats. Very often people keep these coats in their bedroom closet. It really robs you of valuable space.

Be sure you go through all the winter items you keep here. People tend to have far too many winter coats. If the shelf above allows, have baskets for hats, gloves, mittens, and scarves. You'll be able to grab everything as you exit your home. During the warm months, you can move these to that extra shelf I hope you're installing in every closet.

Containers and baskets vary in style and type. You can find plastic, wicker, rattan, and bamboo, just to name the most popular. You'll find containers with and without lids. Here I would use lids and keep them on the top shelf. When the cold weather ends, those gloves and scarves you won't use for a few months not only can go up on the top shelf, but they also can be covered and protected from dust. A few cedar chips are a good idea if you have woolens.

Floor space here is usually at a premium because this is, by nature, not a large closet. I would use the wide wooden shoe rack, if you can. Some families keep small mats by the front door and let their wet shoes dry here before they put them away. If the winter is brutal, they may stay out till spring.

If you live in a milder climate and have no hall closet, take heart. A clothes tree near the front door will hold your heavier coats and those of your guests. In a mild climate, we tend to have more jackets and blazers. These can have a section in your clothes closet. For some reason, in milder climates, the hall closet vanishes and the master closet increases in size.

If you have a few feet of wall space by the front door, you can put a long piece of furniture here, preferably with a few deep cubbyholes or drawers. A mirror is often placed above this so you can give your appearance a quick check as you leave the house. In the Chinese art of feng shui, this mirror by the door represents prosperity. I call this the ultimate win/win situation.

Linen Closets

As we come to the end of this chapter, we must consider the linen closet. If yours allows, keep sheet set sizes together on particular shelves. This way, everyone knows where the twin, double, queen, and/or king sets are. If you have children, keeping your sheets and pillowcases in neat stacks may be difficult. Try these tricks: use shelf dividers between sets and/or put an entire set inside one of its pillowcases.

If you have towel sets, you might want them here as well. Generally, we have one bath sheet or large towel, two hand towels, and a washcloth in each set. I stack my sets and keep them in color order. Use shelf dividers if you want; they make life easier. You may want to keep your towel sets in your bathroom. We'll discuss this in the chapter on bathroom decluttering. If you have space that works well, each bathroom can have its own personal supply of towels.

If your towel sets are in the bathrooms, the linen closet can be where you keep your beach towels or those you use to clean your animals. My golden retriever has his own towels. Don't forget to try space bags for summer storage of extra blankets. Items that lie flat work best in the bags. Things like pillows may break the seal on your space bag as they try to fluff up; it's the nature of the beast.

The Least You Need to Know

- Keeping your clothing organized by color and type will make getting dressed a breeze.

- The right tools (shoe racks, storage boxes, wall hooks, and so on) can make a difficult closet work without having to spend thousands on a remodel.

- The past will not return, no matter how long you hold on to sentimental garments you can no longer wear. Donate them to a charity and enjoy your tax deduction.

- If you're vertically challenged, by all means, have a step stool in your closet.

- Pack those items that you want to store in a closet in appropriate containers, and label them clearly.

Bathrooms: Come Clean—Are They a Great Escape?

In This Chapter

- ◆ Learn tips and tricks to make use of every square inch of your bathroom
- ◆ Organize your bathroom supplies so you can save time in the morning
- ◆ Teach your children how to navigate in the bathroom without creating clutter
- ◆ Make your guests feel welcome

Some people really know how to turn a bathroom into an oasis where they can regularly recharge their batteries. Others use the bathroom in a purely utilitarian way. And then there are those for whom this chapter is written. See if any of the following statements ring true for you:

- I'd like to take a relaxing bath but can't seem to make the time.

- The bathroom has been overrun by the kids. I feel like I'm at Disneyland.

- My bathroom is so tiny, I can't do anything with it. There's just enough room for me to turn around!

- We have such a large bathroom, I don't know how to set it up. There always seems to be a big mess on the counters.

Assessment: What's Here and What Tools Do I Need?

Let's start with the master bath. Once you fix that, you'll know pretty much how to fix every bathroom in your home. Traditionally, it's not a large room with multiple tasks, so the learning curve is easy and less complicated than dealing with a closet or the kitchen.

First, let's pinpoint the biggest clutter culprits. See if this list covers it for you:

Timely Tidbits

If you have more towels than bars to hang them on, it isn't expensive or time-consuming to put up a few hooks in the bathroom. You don't even need hardware. You can use the peel-and-stick variety. Be warned: you can't move these without affecting the paint, so place them carefully the first time.

- Are towels constantly strewn about the floor?

- Are lotions, potions, makeup, and shaving gear left on the counter in the morning?

- Do Fifi and Fido deposit hair all over the floor, especially during shedding season?

- Do the kids prefer your bathroom and leave their things here?

- Do you find yourself complaining about one particular thing when it comes to this room?

Make a list in your faithful *Declutter Notebook* of all the things that create clutter and drive you crazy. Let our list of questions be your inspiration. Be concise. Grab some of your trusty heavy-duty garbage bags. And, last but not least, don't forget to create a shopping list, in case you find you need some organizing items.

The Quick Fix

Want to keep the bathroom looking clutter-free? Always re-hang your towel after each use. If there are dirty towels on the floor, pick them up and put them in the hamper. If the room isn't big enough for a hamper, you'll need one in the bedroom that this bathroom services, or in that bedroom's closet.

Towels are usually damp when they hit the hamper, so it's nice to have one in the bathroom dedicated to this task. You can find great ones for this purpose that allow air to flow so you don't get mold and mildew. No space? Just let the dirty towels dry and then put them in the hamper.

Bathroom drawers are usually chaotic and a bit scary. Let's work our way down the rows. (I presume that you have a few drawers.) Toss any old, expired, no-longer-used and/or wanted prescriptions, makeup, lotions, potions, condoms, bath oils, and any other category unique to you.

Timely Tidbits

If you have a large stash of perfectly good items you tried once and decided not to use (think shampoo or body lotion) and feel guilty tossing them, why not have some friends over for a product swap party?

Ladies, let's be realistic about the number of nail polish bottles, lipstick tubes, combs, brushes, and blow dryers you really need. If your search for the best hair products has seen you amass a collection greater than Beyoncé's, lose the ones you no longer use. Gentlemen, if you have squeezed that toothpaste tube until it's hollered, toss it.

Use your counter as a work space or, if it's too small, spread some towels on the floor before you start. While you're tossing, sort and create categories for anything that's staying.

Let's look under the sink. We all like to have some extras here of the items common to all the occupants of the room: hand and/or body soap, toilet paper, drain opener, toothpaste, and so on. It's nice to have one item in use and one spare in this room. Just be sure that, in an effort to stay stocked, you don't go overboard and create clutter. If you don't have extra storage, see if you can store your additional supplies on an extra shelf in a nearby closet. Get rid of packaging wherever you can. For example, you need the tube of toothpaste or the bottle of shampoo, not the boxes they came in.

Timely Tidbits

Let your medicine chest be just that: a place to store prescription medicines. Carefully choose the other items you want to have here. If you don't use something every day, store it away.

Finally, let's clean out the medicine cabinet. Again, if medications or other items have expired or aren't used any longer, start pitching.

Some people have large bathrooms and the luxury of extra cabinets. Clean out those areas as well. We're paring to the stuff you really use.

Key Items

Once your shelves and drawers are clear, you will want to wipe them out and possibly line them, as you did in the kitchen.

Next, take a look at your categories: do some items belong in the drawers? Do you need small containers to keep them separate and tidy between uses? Remember, you can try a new pattern in the liner or a different material for the drawer inserts.

Are there items you habitually keep on the countertop? Are you attached to having them there? Go to your favorite organizing store or peruse their website, and see if you can find special containers. For example, there are wonderful Lucite holders for lipsticks, cotton swabs, cotton balls, toothpaste, and toothbrushes that look lovely on the counter—provided, of course, that you have the room. If it's going to be crowded, you're creating a new kind of clutter.

Perilous Pitfalls

Just like in the kitchen, if you have small children, keep a childproof lock on the bathroom cabinet door. You don't want little ones getting into cleaners and other bathroom supplies.

Some categories, like hair-care products, are best housed in square containers with handles. If you have a deep drawer or extra space under the sink, you can simply pull out your container when it's time to do your hair, for example, and then put everything away in one quick motion.

The best containers for the bathroom are made from plastic because they're easy to wipe out. You'll find that these containers also come in mesh. Traditionally, there are two sizes: a small square and a larger container that's a rectangle. If you share your bathroom, you may each want to have a different color or type of container to further demarcate your product.

So what does belong in this room? Here is a basic list to which you can add or delete categories, depending on your unique needs. A person with a long-term illness, for example, has special needs, as do those with physical disabilities. This is for the mainstream:

- Hair-care products (shampoo, conditioner, mousse, gel, comb, brushes, and appliances like a hair dryer, hot rollers, a curling iron, and so on)

- Makeup for ladies

- Shaving needs for men

- Body-care products

- Prescriptions

- Dental products

- Eye-care products

- Feminine hygiene products

- Nail-care products

- General first aid

- Cold and flu remedies

- Condoms

Timely Tidbits

If counter space is abundant, feel free to have a few containers out. Be sure you are consistent with the style and color. Acrylic, bamboo, glass, or chrome containers are all great choices. When you mix and match, however, you run the risk of creating visual clutter.

From Help to Hindrance: A Special Kind of Decluttering

Oddly enough, over the years, I have seen a unique form of clutter in many bathrooms. When someone has died after a long illness, those left behind frequently hold on to the special items that were purchased for the care of the terminal member of the household. These items are best donated to a friend or family member in a similar situation or to a retirement home, long-term-care facility, or similar facility. You needn't return from the funeral and do this the same day. However, if it has been more than six months or a year, consider cleansing the environment of these reminders of a difficult time.

This attachment may also come up for those who have suffered through long-term care after an accident. For example, I broke my foot a little more than a year ago. I had to buy a special seat for my shower, waterproof tape, a walking boot, a walker, a cane, and so on. Many people told me to save these items so that if I needed them in the future, I would be prepared. I prefer to think that I will be healthy and know that if I need these items again, they will be available for me to purchase or borrow from friends. I happily donated them all to a church. I can't mandate what is right for you; I can only share that just looking at these things made me sad and uncomfortable.

> **Timely Tidbits**
>
> It can be freeing to clean out special-care items like crutches, bandages, or pain medications that are no longer needed. Why keep them and remind yourself of past injuries? Think healthy, and declutter!

Cupboards and Drawers: Divide and Conquer

I think you will find that once you eliminate the clutter you have allowed to collect over the years and divide your products into categories, you will be well on your way to having order in this room. Everyday items like toothpaste, brushes, floss, and so on generally live in one of the small top drawers. Take a good look at your categories and ask yourself what else you use every day. These items should live in the bathroom proper. Allow the others to migrate outside the room, if necessary.

For example, if you have your nails done every six months and don't have the drawer space, perhaps you can put these supplies elsewhere. Sometimes an extra shelf in the nearest closet yields space. I also find space in the linen closet, which may accommodate a new shelf.

 **Timely Tidbits**

The ability to use products in clever and unique ways that even the manufacturer didn't envision is one of the elements that make getting organized so creative.

In all the years I have been organizing, I have seen only one bathroom that was so tiny it literally held nothing. The sink was a pedestal with no cupboard or counter, and there was no wall space for a shelf. I had to be very creative to make this bathroom work for this poor lady. This was a small apartment on the ocean that was originally part of a home. It was never meant to stand alone.

We got a heavy-duty plastic unit on wheels that had four drawers—the same unit I suggest in the chapter on closets for extra clothing or to use in a child's room to store toys. Remember, a good organizing tool can have many applications. In fact, you know where I can always find this item? At office-supply stores! If you have a desk with no drawers, this can be your solution.

This unit gave my client the drawers she lacked; she could just wheel it in when she needed to. In addition, we put some categories in containers and placed those on one of the shelves in the linen closet. It was huge and right outside the tiny bathroom. The containers went in with her in the morning. They held makeup and hair-care products. The rolling unit had items she might not need every single day.

Adding Space for Storage

Yesterday I was in the bathroom of a new office. My client had just moved in, and we were creating a shopping list of items she needed to make the office work well. The bathroom is small, and at first we thought of buying one of those units that goes above the toilet.

As a facility for the public, it needs two handicap rails. We realized we had to place the toilet seat cover dispenser, the paper towel dispenser, the wastebasket, and the soap dispenser. We decided that the extra storage unit would just make clutter. Last evening, my client's handyman installed the necessities and then hung two art pieces. The bathroom is now beautiful, functional, and clutter-free.

Is there too much in your bathroom? Do you need to add things for storage, or will you be maxing out the space and making it feel claustrophobic? Do you have pretty countertop items or nice hooks or perhaps some wall space for a framed poster? A bathroom needs to be functional but it can also have a personality.

Where's My Robe?

One thing it's nice to have immediate access to is your robe. I would say the world is divided into two camps: those who put a hook or two on the back of the bathroom door so their robes are always handy, and those who keep their robes on hooks or hangers in the closet. Do whatever feels right. My robe is in the bathroom behind the door. I have my pjs or nightgown on another hanger. I'm set when it comes time to get ready for bed.

Counter Culture

A clean, clear bathroom counter is a wonderful sight to behold. To be sure, you can find beautiful products out there that can dress up the room if you do have lots of space. I am thinking of Q-tip dispensers, display trays, and makeup and lipstick holders, all meant to beautify the room and keep things convenient for you. It just depends on your counter space and how often you need these items.

Ladies very often have a small container on the counter that holds their everyday jewelry. No matter how much we have, we seem to wear the same things day in and day out. Mine is a small wooden box given to me by dear friends one year for my birthday. I get to remember them every morning when I take out my favorite jewelry for another day. Two other categories I see in clients' homes are the electric toothbrush that needs to charge all the time and one or more beautiful perfume bottles. Again, take a hard look at the space and ask yourself whether you are adding or distracting with the items you want out.

The World of Fragrance

Speaking of perfumes, I must confess that, like many people, I love fragrances—not just those I wear personally, but beautiful bath products that make my bathroom smell like paradise. These can be in the form of soaps, bath oils, bath crystals, incense sticks, even candles. If you really love this form of expression, you might think about introducing some products to the rest of the house. Perhaps you'll want to have signature scents in different rooms? Lavender is traditional in the bedroom because it promotes sleep, while citrus in the kitchen or dining room is great because it can make us think about eating.

Remember that oils must be stored out of direct sunlight, and no products retain their fragrance forever. Don't overbuy and then have to toss things in a few months without having enjoyed them. Be sure to ask those with whom you share your space if they have the same love of the scents you are using. You don't want this to backfire! I had a client who always smelled great. One day she told me her husband was allergic to fragrance. I asked her how she managed to smell so good all the time. She laughed and told me she put it on after he left for work. It was gone by the time he returned home in the evening!

Tell-Tale Towels

How often you change your towels is a personal matter. How many you use should be dictated by the space in the bathroom. Shelves enable you to keep extras out at all times. Towel bars are also helpful. If you lack either of these, it doesn't take much time or expense to install some extras. Hooks can hold the towels you are currently using.

Many of my clients keep the area under the sink for extra hand towels and face cloths because they use several each day. You want to be sure you can get things out easily, which is why I love using containers there. Remember that the area under the sink is subject to leaks. Be sure it's organized so your plumber can get in and out of there easily and you won't regret losing any items if they are damaged. Extra shampoo bottles are expendable in an emergency. Losing expensive Egyptian cotton hand towels is another story.

If you have a small bathroom, you may want to use the large towel just under a bath sheet. The latter is wonderful because you can wrap yourself in it while you are putting on your makeup or shaving. The downside is that it takes up a lot more room. I can't resist saying it here: less is once again more!

Kids' Bathrooms: SpongeBob to iPod

Like the bedroom, a child's bathroom should be a fun place. If several children have to share this room, be sure the little ones can have their special bath toys without making the older ones feel that SpongeBob has invaded! If the shower and the tub are separate, for example, you could put up a toy hammock above the tub. You could also have a special container to hold the bath treasures.

As children grow, remember that the décor has to keep pace with their changing needs. SpongeBob may give way to a racing shower curtain. Barbie dolls may go away and be replaced by iPods and makeup that the current pop queen uses. Sometimes parents see the physical changes in their children and don't realize they are holding on to their children through their environment.

Reach for the Counter, Dive into the Drawers

A small step stool made for a child (a heavier one that is unlikely to tip over) is a great addition to this room. It's so important to be able to reach the sink and wash your hands by yourself, isn't it? Be sure your child's products are set up in drawers and cupboards, just like yours are. Seeing the same setup as Mom and Dad have will make your child feel grown-up. If you keep your drawers and cupboards tidy, it will be easier to demand the same of your child.

Guest Bath: Would You Feel Welcome?

If you love to buy small sizes of products or if you travel a lot and have a stash from airlines, why not create a guest welcome basket? Tell your guests they don't have to bring the basics, like toothpaste or deodorant, because you'll supply these for them. Those small items add up and really weight down a bag. If you're one of those busy execs who have acquired tons of small product sizes from first-class travel, take what you want for yourself and your guests, and donate the rest to a women's shelter.

If your guest is sharing the bathroom you also use, be sure you give your guest your work hours before he or she arrives so you can set your schedules. The same idea goes if a guest has to share a bathroom with a child. I have had to do that in several homes. I always get the school or work schedule the night before. Can you imagine being late because your guest is taking a bubble bath?

Rituals: The Power of Fun

Everyone needs to recharge. Oddly, we almost always have to be reminded to do so. It's especially critical if you are a working parent. Be sure you schedule a little "rest and relaxation" (R&R) for yourself. If you don't replenish yourself, how will you have anything to give?

My idea of a treat happens once a month. I light candles with a favorite fragrance. I dim the lights and soak for 20 minutes in a hot tub. Like the idea but have no spouse to help with the kids? When your friends ask what you want for your birthday, tell them to come over and watch the kids. You would treasure 30 uninterrupted minutes alone. This, of course, is my ritual. You can exercise your creativity and make up your own ritual.

Aftermath

More than any other room in the home, the bathroom requires a special kind of daily maintenance. You may have to create some new habits. Instead of going on the floor, dirty towels now go on a hook or into a hamper. Makeup no longer free-floats in a drawer with rollers and a hair dryer. There is a place for everything, and everything must indeed go back to that designated place. This room is usually small, so it isn't as forgiving when we don't honor the new system; it takes only one morning, rather than a few days, for a lack of attention to be obvious.

Beyond these concerns, however, are things like sticky counters and hair flowing across the floor like tumbleweeds. As you leave your bathroom after your morning ritual, remember to wipe off the counter. You can use a wet sponge or one of those pop-up sheets with disinfectant. Special types of floor cleaners will grab hair easily and instantly. Swiffer makes one that's easy to stow and works well.

I have a golden retriever, and I swear I could make a puppy at least once a week with the hair that my boy deposits on my bathroom floor! He keeps me on my toes. If you have a cat and keep your litter box here, you will want to clean up the fallout from the litter box regularly. Ever exit the shower and step barefoot on litter gravel? Again, you can use your Swiffer or a Dustbuster to work wonders. Whatever your choices are for maintenance, just remember to do them regularly.

The Least You Need to Know

♦ You can always examine the bathroom to see if some simple additions, like a towel bar, hook, or shelf, will make the room work better.

♦ At best, this isn't a huge room, so you have to pare the contents and keep the resulting categories in designated places.

♦ Bathrooms require more than faithful adherence to the new system you put in place. They require daily cleaning rituals.

♦ Never forget the power of the bathroom as a place to restore your tired body and soul. Can you say bubble bath?

Home Office: How Should You Set It Up?

In This Chapter

♦ Create a file system that supports your household/business activities

♦ Tailor the physical setup of a room to your individual business needs

♦ Lessen the load when you leave your home and still have everything you need

♦ Harness time so that it becomes your friend and helps you reach your goals

From my perspective, working at home has more advantages than disadvantages. For me, the biggest drawback is the temptation to sneak into the office "after hours" and work till dawn, when I should be in bed getting some much-needed sleep. The biggest advantages are being able to work in my pjs, if I choose, and not having to face the freeways of Los Angeles during rush hour.

My situation is unique, since I run a home-based business. You may not need or have a separate room for such an endeavor. Therefore, the best way to use this chapter is to read it in its entirety and then pick and choose the information and tips that help you create a custom solution for your personal setup at home.

Assessment: What's Here and What Tools Do I Need?

If you're like me and you're fond of the bottom line, here it is: have in your office only the things you really need. A scanner is a great technological toy, for example, and these are incredibly affordable right now. However, do you need one? How often will you use it? If you have a computer, you'll need a printer. You can buy them now for a song, but if you get an inkjet printer, the ink cartridges will drive you to the poorhouse if you print frequently. On the other hand, a laser printer is expensive up front but saves you money in the long haul. This kind of critical thinking is required for every facet of your setup.

Here is a list of questions for your *Declutter Notebook*. Let's devise a plan tailored to your needs:

- ◆ What do you need to accomplish in this work space?

- ◆ Do you have the technological tools you need? For example, does your desktop need an upgrade?

- ◆ Would DSL or cable modem facilitate your work in this room?

- ◆ Is it time to go wireless?

- ◆ Could you move from desktop to laptop? You may want to consult a computer expert. He will also be able to advise you on the software programs that may assist you.

- ◆ Do you have a file cabinet or file container of some sort for your work?

- ◆ Do you have all the file supplies you need? (We deal with this later, in case you are clueless in this area.)

- ◆ Is your desk the right size?

♦ Do you have a comfortable chair? One on wheels is a bonus, as is one of those office mats underneath to let you move easily.

♦ Is a space available for archived files? (Again, more information about this appears shortly. Don't panic!)

Timely Tidbits _____

If possible, place your file cabinet near your desk so that you can slide over to get whatever you need. Steps saved equal time saved.

If the room is used for other purposes, what is the most important use of the space? If it's your work, do you need to downsize other elements in the room? For example, is it time to sell or store the queen-size bed and get a futon for guests? Have you joined a gym, and could your equipment be sold on eBay or Craig's List?

The Quick Fix

In almost every chapter of this book, a quick fix is possible in about an hour. This room may provide you with more of a challenge. You may need to plot your way to success over the course of several days. Creating a home office isn't like tossing old, unidentifiable frozen meat. It takes creativity and craft. This chapter appears late in this book so that you can ideally approach it after getting some good declutter experience under your belt. It takes time for clutter to accumulate. It stands to reason that it may take some time to make it disappear. The key is that you have started.

If this room's purpose is confused—is it a guest room, home office, or gym?—you'll need to decide if it's serving all those functions or is so full of stuff that it's serving no purpose. Your first task is to work on the physical setup. Depending on how cluttered it is, here are the steps you may need to follow to achieve success. Add or delete to suit your situation.

1. Remove any clutter that can be either trashed outright (reinforced trash bags, anyone?), donated, recycled, or moved to another part of the house.

2. If there is a closet, make sure it's organized. For a home office, it's ideal if this closet can just be a supply area. You can have shelves

built for office supplies or go to a home store and purchase an inexpensive bookcase. Voilà! You now have instant shelves at your disposal.

3. If you are going to make this a multipurpose room, be sure each activity has its own area. Do you have what you need for each?

The minimum for a successful home office these days is a good-size desk; a comfortable chair; a file cabinet; good lighting (overhead or lamps); and an electronic setup to suit your needs: computer or laptop, monitor (flat screens take up less room), phone, bookcase, and any other equipment you will use, like a fax or scanner. With identity theft a growing industry, every office needs a shredder. Shredding as you go saves time in the long run.

Once the physical setup is ready, it's time to dive into the world of paper. Your file system is key to your success. If you work it, you can kiss paper clutter goodbye.

A Sea of Paper

I'd like you to create a workspace for this part of the project. Let's clear off your desk or, if you need it and have one, set up a folding table as a temporary staging area. No matter how many piles or stacks of paper you have and no matter how close to the ceiling they go, we're going to look at only one at a time. Let's say 12 inches high is our max, okay?

Here are some questions to help you blast through your piles, one piece of paper at a time. By the way, look at the papers just long enough to identify them. Now is not the time to stop and read magazines or linger over vacation photos. You need to keep moving! See things you meant to take care of weeks ago? Start a section called "To Do" and take care of business later. Here are your key questions:

♦ Do I need this? If not, toss it.

♦ Is this information now available on the Internet? If so, toss it.

♦ Is someone else in the family or organization saving this information? If so, do you have access upon demand? Yes? Toss your copy. (You can also use this setup in your regular office, and apply it to school projects or anything that has paper!)

As you find things you *do* need to keep, identify the broad category to which this piece of paper belongs. Keep your categories separate and use post-its to identify them. Here are the most common categories in addition to the just-referenced "To Do" section:

♦ Paid bills

♦ Credit card statements

♦ Bank statements

♦ Investment records

♦ Insurance information

♦ Papers for each child in the family

♦ Material related to hobbies, recipes, travel articles, and more

♦ Old tax returns and the materials that support them

♦ Real estate transactions

> **Timely Tidbits**
>
> Don't let the fear of making a mistake prevent you from tossing papers you think you no longer need. If you're confused, call an expert in that field. Real estate questions? Call your real estate agent. Tax questions? Call your tax preparer. Let the experts be your guide.

The items on your list are unique and personal to you. In fact, this list reflects your life. What matters is that you now gather related papers together. After about an hour, instead of stacks of unrelated papers that make you crazy, you will have neat piles of separate categories. With this step, you are creating the bones of your file system.

> **Timely Tidbits**
>
> Categories enable us to instantly see all the information we have on a particular topic. This makes our work time easier and more productive.

Too Many Magazines Spoil the Area

Do you have subscriptions to lots of magazines? For many people, parting with old issues is just that—an issue. The reality is, if you haven't made time to read a magazine in a month, you probably aren't ever going to make the time.

If it's a magazine with pretty pictures of fashion or decorating and you flipped through it when it arrived, guess what? You got your money's worth. Just remember what that latte costs you at the local coffee shop and how quickly it's consumed. Pleasure is fleeting. Don't demand too much bang for your buck.

See an article you want to read? Take it out and create a "To Read" pile. You can tear out the article or use a special magazine clipper. I like to tear the magazine itself apart along its spine. You'll get perfectly clean margins this way. If you need to keep the article and it's long, cut away all extraneous material and staple the parts together. One or two tiny articles of importance are very often buried in a stack of magazines and newspapers. Bring everything down to its least common denominator. Here size matters: the smaller, the better.

Timely Tidbits

Never create a file for just one piece of paper. If no other information is coming regarding this topic, have a "Miscellaneous" file into which you place all these orphan papers.

I rarely keep back issues for more than two months—a year, at most. There are all manner of magazine holders; some are heavy-duty cardboard, others are luxurious leather. You decide what works best in your office. We want everything you keep to be accessible, not in another pile.

When you bring in your newspaper, the first thing you should do is eliminate any sections you aren't going to read. If you don't read the newspaper during the course of the day, toss it. Old news is just that.

Don't forget that many magazines and newspapers are now offered online. If you feel you must save them, burn them on CDs to be read later.

Who Needs This?

As you move through your piles, you will probably discover items that belong to other members of your family. Create a category or stack of papers for each person in your household. As you come across photos and memorabilia items, put them aside as separate categories. More about them in a minute.

Following these steps will help you make sense of the papers on your table.

What Happens to My Stacks?

Your stacks will show you in black and white the interests and details that make up your life. Most people are surprised to find that their lives are not as complicated as they imagined. Whenever all of your papers are jumbled together, it can seem as if the sum of the parts of our life is one overwhelming mess. You're about to get control.

I am going to take you through a few of the most common categories to show you how to break down each stack into its logical parts and then organize them so that you achieve two goals:

1. You can easily find whatever you need.

2. You know exactly where to put whatever comes in.

Are you ready? Follow these steps to success. Take a look at all your stacks. Do you see that some are related? For example, perhaps you are taking a trip to China this year and next year you are planning to go to Europe. These two areas are far apart on the globe, but they are related under the umbrella of travel. Label a tab on a hanging folder as "Travel." Inside include a folder for China and then one for Europe. Within each category, keep everything in alphabetical order.

Timely Tidbits

When the room begins to fill with trash bags, stop and take them to your garbage can or dumpster. Too many items in a room can leave you feeling overwhelmed. As the room clears, you'll have a better sense of what you have accomplished.

Timely Tidbits

If you have many documents that need to be shredded, consider hiring your teenager or a neighbor to do the job for you. As I noted earlier, every office needs a shredder, and your teenager can do the work under your supervision. In addition, if you have boxes of paper to be shredded, licensed and bonded services will pick them up and shred them for you. Consult your Yellow Pages.

Time to File

Let's get all your related piles near each other. Remember, I didn't say mix them—just place them in the same geographical area. In this way, a typical person's papers break down like this:

◆ **Family** is in one area. These are items like the medical files for you and your children, all household bills, automotive and DMV papers, children's school records, and legal docs for the family, like passports and birth certificates.

◆ **Work** is everything related to your work, whether it's done outside the home or in this office.

◆ All your **hobbies and interests** can be in one section.

◆ An **everyday** stack or two consists of things you need to accomplish to keep your life running.

When you have your groups established, you will have an idea of how many file drawers you need. Everyday business is best kept near you. I like to use simple manila folders for this material. If you run a business, you will want these folders together in another drawer or two, or three, depending on their volume. I like to designate a special color for business files. Finally, your family and personal interests can share a drawer, depending on the size of the categories and the number of file drawers you have.

> **Timely Tidbits**
>
> Using colored folders to identify projects on sight can save you time when you have multiple project files on your desk and you need to locate something quickly.

In the front of the drawer where you have your everyday business files, begin with a section called "Action Files." These are the ones you touch and deal with on a daily basis:

◆ Bills

◆ To Call

◆ To Do: ASAP

◆ To Do: Low Priority

- ◆ To File
- ◆ To Read

I use box bottom hanging folders to help me save space in the drawer and time when I am searching for something. This is a hanging folder with a piece of cardboard on the bottom. I like the 2-inch-wide variety myself. If you get wider ones, you can

Perilous Pitfalls

People often think the lines at the bottom of a regular hanging folder are where you can make creases and get more folders inside. Doing this shortens the hanging folder, and the individual files you put inside will stick up and prevent the drawer from closing.

put more files inside, but the weight of the paper usually breaks the box bottom in short order. All of the materials I just mentioned go in individual manila folders inside the box bottom—notice that I kept the alphabetical order.

Bills

When bills come in, some people pay everything on the first and/or the fifteenth of the month. The day the bill arrives, I make a note in my Day Runner calendar on when I need to pay each bill. I put the payment coupon here along with the envelope if I mail in my payment. If I am paying online, I don't need the envelope. I file the rest of the bill because, with a home-based business, most of my expenses are tax-deductible. The ads and the used envelope get tossed. I am constantly eliminating and reducing every aspect of my life to the bottom line.

You can handle bill paying in several ways. If you have the means and know you are forgetful in this area, you can have most of your bills paid automatically. This works for payment amounts that are static, like a car or house payment. You can also turn over this task to a bookkeeper or CPA and review the monthly statement to be sure everything is in order. Perhaps you have a spouse and one of you is better at finances than the other. There are lots of ways to tackle this issue. The bottom line is that you want to pay on time so that your credit rating keeps going up.

Time-Management Tools

In passing, I mentioned that I use the Day Runner calendar. This has been my brand of choice for more than 20 years. I use the Entrepreneur edition because the pages are larger. You can create a system that's unique to you and your needs by choosing just the right insert pages for your calendar. For example, I use the "month at a glance" pages because I like to be sure I am balancing my time between work and play. If I see only one day at a time, I can get lost in the moment and overschedule myself. Here is where you have to get the material that's right for you. Once again, this is where getting organized and decluttering your life gets to be creative and fun.

Focus on Filing

On the left side of a hanging folder, I attach a tab. This tab announces a category change. If my category is complicated and large, I might need several hanging folders. It's okay to use a mixture of box bottom and regular. Just be sure to keep your tabs in a single row. Staggering tabs looks sloppy and creates visual clutter.

"To Do" Files

Very often, a piece of paper, such as a letter from a company you are doing business with, will require you to write a response or make a phone call. Perhaps you returned an item and want to know when your account will be credited. Or perhaps you lodged a complaint in a return letter and are now waiting for a response.

Perilous Pitfalls

Box bottom hanging folders can't be used without the cardboard insert on the bottom. They will be too long and will drag on the floor of the file drawer.

You can keep these materials in your "To Do" folder; when the folder gets thinner, you know you have made progress. What to do? Create a "Pending" folder. Put this behind your "Action" section in a separate hanging folder. Place a tab called "Pending" on the right side of that hanging folder. Now when you open the drawer, you know that all your master categories are announced by the tabs on the left and all subcategories are indicated by the tabs on the right.

Family Business Files

Let's take a look at your family business materials. Let me see how many I can guess. Here's my list:

- ◆ **Automobile:**
  DMV
  Payments/lease
  Tickets/traffic court

- ◆ **Business expenses:**
  Dues
  Entertaining
  Periodicals (research material)
  Travel expenses

- ◆ **Credit cards:**
  AMEX
  MasterCard
  Visa
  Department store cards

- ◆ **Medical:**
  Claim forms
  Policy information
  Pending claims (Most people like to keep these separate from the general "Pending" folder. The choice is yours.)

- ◆ **Mortgage payment (or rent)**

- ◆ **Phones:**
  Business line
  Cellphone
  Fax
  Home

◆ **Utilities:**
Electric
Gas
Water

This is just a sample. The top line represents the category or tab name, and the list that follows is the individual folders making up that category. Follow this pattern to get your individual family folders in order. If you have several children, you may want to create a section for them. Each child would then have the same folders, thus keeping their individual information separated.

◆ **Annie:**
Immunization record
School report cards
Sports:
Horseback riding
Soccer

◆ **Joseph:**
Immunization record
School report cards
Sports:
Baseball
Football

◆ **Lynn:**
Immunization record
School report cards
Sports:
Swimming

Legal Files

It's wise to keep family legal documents together. I simply create a file called "Legal Documents." This way, when you get a last-minute request for a child's birth certificate or need your passport, you're set. There is only one place to look!

Cooking and Traveling Files

Many people have recipes and travel articles. These are also categories that are often dumped into a drawer and then never accessed.

I would divide the recipes just as you might find them in a cookbook:

- Appetizers
- Breads
- Soups
- Poultry
- Fish
- Meat

- Vegetarian meals
- Potato dishes
- Pasta, rice, and grains
- Salads
- Desserts

For travel, divide it by area of the world you want to visit. You might have these categories:

- Africa/Safari
- Asia
- Europe
- South America
- USA: by state or city (in alphabetical order, of course!)

Timely Tidbits

If you put your file list on your computer, you can keep a hard copy on your desk in a small binder with other "reference" material. Now when you wonder where a file is, your fingers can literally do the walking and tell you where to find it.

Don't forget to create a section for your home city so that you can get to know it better over time. Even if you grew up there, this will keep you from being bored. For example, I have a section for Los Angeles and New York that has the following folders for each city:

- Places of interest
- Restaurants (to try)

Warranties and Manuals

Do you have an empty drawer filled with warranties and instruction manuals? Do you dread when something breaks or you have to research something because you know it will take an hour to find the material? Are some of the manuals separate because you want to keep them near the equipment they came with? Stop the madness! I divide all of my warranties and manuals by the overall category and file them accordingly. Put them in the back of a drawer you won't access that often. It looks like this:

- ◆ Appraisals/artwork
- ◆ Computer: All related equipment—the CPU, the monitor, the scanner, the CD or DVD burners, and so on
- ◆ Entertainment: TVs/DVD players/VHS players, and so on
- ◆ Household: Vacuum cleaner, furniture receipts, and so on
- ◆ Jewelry
- ◆ Kitchen and laundry: Appliances (oven, refrigerator, washer, dryer) and cooking aids (grill, waffle maker, iron)

See how absolutely every category can be broken down into the parts that make it whole?

Archival Files

Inevitably, we all have information we need to keep; however, it doesn't have to be at our fingertips. We have to save our income tax returns forever. Why not have an archival file cabinet or container to house them? This is a good place for the back-up material we have to keep for a few years. (Check with your tax preparer for the latest rules.) Remember, these are business archives, not memorabilia.

Create Your Office Environment

Don't forget that, along with utility, beauty is an important consideration in setting up your office. Here are some things you can do:

- Paint the walls a relaxing color.

- Have some easy-care plants.

- Be sure you have a music source, if this helps you work more effectively.

- Water fountains are popular today. You might find putting one just inside the door is soothing. You can put it on a small table, or you can purchase one of the wall fountains that are quite smart-looking. If you run a home-based business, you may be interested to know that in traditional feng shui, this water in the entry should bring increased wealth. And you thought all Chinese restaurants had fish tanks because they love fish!

- Hang things on the wall that you find inspiring.

Office Supplies

There's no question that I have my favorite office supplies. Here's my list. What would you add or subtract?

- Manila folders

- Colored folders

- Hanging folders (to house the manila or colored folders)

- Extra-long file tabs

- Box bottom hanging folders (to help you keep large categories together)

- Pens and pencils (I use felt-tip pens and automatic pencils)

- Post-it notes (they come in different sizes, though I prefer the medium size)

- Scissors

- Tape and dispenser

- Paper clips (I like colorful ones, large and small)

- Stapler and staples

- Ruler

- Glue stick

- Extra erasers

- One or two highlighters in different colors

- A label maker and extra cassettes (black letters on a white background works best)

Is It a Lilliputian Desk or a Gunboat?

The size of your desk is dictated by many things, including the size of the room and what you intend to do here. Be sure you have a writing surface. If the keyboard and computer monitor hog the desk, try to put them on a return so you can use the desk proper to spread out your papers when you are working on a project. If you don't have a return built into your desk, you can create one by placing the monitor and keyboard on a separate unit to the side, preferably one on wheels.

Some of my clients get a big desk for a small price by purchasing a simple door at their local home store. You can have the wood finished or painted to suit the decor in the room. All of your computer and telephone wires can be dropped through the opening for the doorknob. The trick is to put the door or a simple piece of lumber on top of two file cabinets. You can get the cabinets with a top drawer and a file drawer. Or you can use the ones with two file drawers and then have a rolling drawer unit (the one we used in your child's room and in your closet) for supplies. These solutions are meant to spark your creativity.

It's popular today to have the computer hidden inside an armoire. This is certainly practical if you just want to stop by and pay bills, check e-mail, and perhaps dash off the occasional letter. I don't care for this setup because, inevitably, you will find yourself with your back to the door. It's better to sit facing the door, especially if you are a fan of feng shui.

Modern Technology

Some of the most well-educated people I know are afraid to touch a computer. They are convinced that they will either never learn how to use it correctly or they will break it. If you are in this category, take heart.

I am a technological moron, yet I can write books on my computer; I surf the web daily and couldn't live without my e-mail. Sometimes I think about all the things my computer can do that I have no clue how to harness. It doesn't matter. It serves me. Make it serve you!

If you love photography and have hesitated to go digital, let me just say that it really can offer you a new world. You can save photos at online sites and even create cyberalbums to share with family and friends. If you choose a photo printer, you can still print hard copies for home albums. Digital cameras are light and easy to use. You get to see your work immediately and can decide on the spot whether you want to delete a shot and move on.

One day I got a new cellphone. It came with a built-in camera. I think it took me two weeks to figure it all out. I watched the 17-year-old daughter of a friend get one of those for Christmas. She had it mastered in about 10 minutes. The best way to learn about new technology, if you aren't near a pro or can't afford a few sessions with one, is to call in a teenager.

A Good Book Is Like an Old Friend ...

A home office is the perfect place to keep the books that relate to your profession. It makes sense to bring business newsletters, periodicals, and newspapers here as well. Many of my clients do not have space for a bookcase in their bedrooms, so they keep personal books here that they do not want to share with others. If you have hobbies and no family room, you might also want to keep those books here as a reference.

Bookcases don't have to be expensive. I frequently shop at Ikea for my clients. Their simple melamine bookcases come in a variety of styles and are reasonably priced. Once they are filled with books, very little of the surface shows. On the bottom shelf, I frequently put magazine holders for the issues I want to keep for reference.

Your upper shelves can be made to look more inviting if you have a few personal pieces out, like an occasional photo, a trip souvenir, or perhaps a few collectibles. I have more than 300 camels, and a few have migrated to my office. It's good to personalize a space and make it more inviting to be there. Be careful you don't cross the line and put out so many things that all you have is clutter.

What's in Your Briefcase Besides a Day-Old Sandwich?

Some professions seem to generate more paper than others. It seems like my attorney and real estate clients, for example, have to carry around more papers than anyone else. It helps to keep the contents of your briefcase lean, pared to exactly what you need.

If you have the luxury of traveling regularly by car, keep a file container in the trunk. For example, here you might keep extra copies of forms or other reference materials that you might need in the field. Be sure the file box has a lid so the papers stay clean. If you're going to take it out and work with it in front of clients, you might want to invest in a hardy material like leather. If it's for your eyes only, a simple plastic file box from your local supply store, like Staples or Office Depot, will do the trick.

These days, a small USB flash-drive that fits on your keychain enables you to take electronic files with you. This saves you having to drag computer disks with you. Look for space savers like these down the line. Many of my clients, for instance, have those zippered containers that have small sizes of the basic office supplies, like staplers and tape dispensers. If you need those things, take one along.

Go through your briefcase and clean it out. When you clear out the clutter, put back only what you need. Very often we feel guilty if we don't have a lot to take with us, and we unconsciously load up the briefcase just so it will be heavy and appear more significant.

Time: Servant or Master?

Entire books have been written about time. We don't have the space to deal with this important topic in detail. Yet I would be remiss if I didn't say a few words about time—it is, after all, the cloth out of which you create your life.

Time is a commodity. It can be squandered, but it can't be saved for later and it can't be replaced. You need to be sure you are charting your course through life rather than living your life constantly in response to others' demands. Here are some key things to remember:

It's okay to say "No"—in fact, it's vital to your survival. You can't respond to every e-mail, voice mail, or snail mail you receive. Nor can you say "Yes" to every request made of you. It sounds obvious, doesn't it? Learning to say "No" takes practice. It's an art that will save you time.

Do you know what your goals are? It's key in life. As you define exactly where you are going in life and what you want you accomplish, every request made of you comes up against your inner guide, who asks, "Does this move me closer to my goal?" If not, be sure you understand why you say "Yes" if you are moved to do so.

I was raised to be a people pleaser. The one thing I have learned is that not only does no one die if I say "No," but people actually respect me more because my "Yes" has more meaning. It's difficult at first. But only at first ….

Aftermath

Few areas in the home require such constant vigilance as the world of paper maintenance. And let's face it, that's what the office is all about. You will need to create positive habits here. Just as you wouldn't leave the house with your teeth unbrushed and your hair a disheveled mess, you can no longer leave the business of your life in the debris of un-organized piles.

No other area of the home has the potential to make you feel so powerful. No other room can move you to your goals quite like this one. Embrace the possibility inherent in the daily changes you will have to make to be successful here. The rewards are remarkable, powerful, and without end. Go for it!

The Least You Need to Know

♦ The home office setup is key to your success here.

♦ A good file system is the guts of the operation.

♦ Material that can be archived should be removed from file cabinets that hold current data.

♦ Beyond the files, the look and feel of the office can make it a welcoming place to spend your time. Add color, plants, even a small fountain.

Chapter **11**

Garage: You Mean My Car Goes Here?

In This Chapter

♦ Learn how storage solutions can help you maximize the space in your garage

♦ Learn how to use storage ideas and containers that stand the test of time

♦ Discover how to use the space available to you here as a de facto extra room

♦ Declutter your car and make it a pleasurable place to spend time

It happens so frequently that I don't know why I am still surprised. I'll be called to a home for one project, typically something mundane, like organizing a closet. In short order, my client decides the entire house needs to be organized. We set up a schedule. As we near the finish line, I hear something along these lines: "I guess you should see the garage. It's a mess out there." *Mess* isn't the word. While the house looks like it's ready to be photographed for a magazine, the poor garage looks like a cyclone hit it. Clutter is only one of the issues. All that clutter is usually dirty as well.

A fix, of course, is always possible. Clutter can't stand in the way of a determined client and a knowledgeable professional organizer! It's sad to see this valuable space so poorly utilized. After all, a garage provides you with extra space and wonderful opportunities for storage. Remember, I said "storage," not "dumping" or "a place to avoid decisions." You know what that's like? It's like getting all dressed up in a beautiful designer gown or tux, but wearing old tattered underwear because "nobody's going to see!" *You* see. And that's what counts.

If you have a garage and you manage to get your car inside, bravo to you! You are in the minority. Your garage may be the first room you see when you get home and the last view of your house as you leave for the day. I think that makes this space very important, don't you? Let's get our *Declutter Notebook* and see what's going on in *your* garage.

Assessment: What's Here and What Tools Do I Need?

The garage clutter I see falls into four general types:

1. First we have the garages that are in cold climates. No matter what else happens here, the car has to fit inside because of the harsh winter weather. The clutter/debris will be pushed up against the walls. It surrounds the vehicle like a frame surrounds a still life.

2. Next we have the typical garage in the temperate zone. It's perfectly fine if the car never sees the inside of this garage. The clutter here oozes into the middle of the garage like gore in a horror movie. No one seems to notice or care because no one ever comes out here except once a year perhaps to fetch Grandma Mae's now-famous holiday roaster.

3. Next we have the benign garage. That's my name for it. This garage is the easiest to fix. It's small and could barely hold a car. It's really meant for seasonal storage, gardening supplies, and other miscellaneous items that don't fit anywhere in the house.

Nothing here really needs to be tossed or donated; it just doesn't have anywhere in the space to go. It's a clutter jumble almost by default.

4. Finally, there's the garage that is "done to the max" just like the house it's attached to. A professional garage or storage company has come out and installed cabinets, hooks, and all the latest bells and whistles. The problem here is that the owners have no idea how to get organized, so everything has just been shoved into the lovely cabinets. They become "keepers of the clutter."

Which garage do you have? Do you have a mixture? Does it change with the seasons? Let's examine the easiest solutions available, and you can pick and choose what works for you.

The Quick Fix

The idea of a quick fix will have to be redefined if you have seriously impacted this space. You can fill your trash cans really quickly, so let's decide first what we need for tools. Take a look around your garage. The first things you want to establish are your goals for the space. Do you need to get the car inside before winter? Has the place been overrun by sporting equipment? Would you like to have a hobby shop out here?

Once you know what your ultimate goals are, you will begin to see the space differently. Your thought process will go something like this: "Gosh, I never thought about a hobby area out here. I could do my scrapbooking/build things/let the kids make a mess right over there … in that far corner … where I have the furniture Aunt Tilly left me 20 years ago. You know, I've never liked that stuff. I need to call a charity and get it out of here." Well, you get the idea. By the way, make a note to call some charities. You need to schedule a pickup day.

Cure for the Worst-Case Scenario

By now, you know that a quick fix is mostly about working the first two steps of The Magic Formula: *eliminate* what no longer serves you and put what remains into *categories*.

Timely Tidbits

When you donate to a charity, be sure you keep a detailed list of the items if you want to take advantage of the tax deduction. Very often the charity will allow you to assign the value of the items. Consult with your tax person, as there are strict guidelines.

Let's make some lists in your *Declutter Notebook*. We'll start with my favorites: "Items to Toss" (larger than those that go into a simple trash bag) and "Items to Donate."

As your first list grows, you may see that you need to rent a bin from a local trash-hauling service. Trash dumpsters usually come in several sizes. Give the company rep an idea of what you have so he can be sure you are on the right track. It's easy to declutter with this tool. The company delivers. You fill the dumpster. They take it away. It's worth its weight in gold.

Be sure you line up some muscle if those items are heavy. No men in the house? Someone in your life must know a few teenage boys who want to make extra money. If you are doing the separating before they arrive and your helpers are only doing the tossing into the bin, be sure you clearly separate items and mark items for the dumpster and the charity from those you are keeping. We don't want Grandma Mae's roaster getting dumped before its time!

Timely Tidbits

A dumpster is a great choice for the person with a garage that is mostly filled with clutter destined for the trash. The minute you start to see dramatic changes in the garage, you're going to be fired up and infused with what I call "completion enthusiasm."

It would be great if the bin arrived the same day the charity came so that you can clear out the big debris all at once. You want to be sure the items you are donating are easy for the charity reps to pick up. Don't count on them to weed through stacks of boxes and debris. When the clutter is gone, you're ready to create categories for everything that's staying.

Let's see how good I am at guessing what's left in your garage:

◆ A folding table and extra chairs for parties

◆ Automotive supplies

- Computer and other equipment (empty) boxes
- Gardening tools and supplies
- Luggage
- Party supplies
- Seasonal decorations
- Sports equipment
- Tools

Timely Tidbits

If you travel frequently, your favorite suitcase is best kept inside your home. Use the garage for those large bags the family needs once a year for the annual holiday.

What's in *your* garage?

The Great Mystery of the Unopened Boxes

Believe it or not, one of the most common forms of garage clutter is a sea of unopened boxes from the last move. While I like the sound of "I haven't seen that stuff in 10 years, so why would I miss it?" I *don't* want you to toss these boxes unopened into the dumpster. Why? Because 6 months or 10 years ago, whenever you packed them, you may have stuck something valuable inside at the last minute to fill up the box. You'll be heartbroken if one day you realize you trashed a treasure.

Open these boxes before the dumpster or the charity arrives. Do whatever you have to do to keep moving: ask a friend to be there, hire a professional organizer, set a timer (say, five minutes maximum per box), or turn on some music with a strong beat. If you find things that belong to members of your family who no longer live at home, call them and tell them what you have. Give them one week to either get the items or send you the money to ship them. Remember, you are retiring as the free off-site storage for everyone you know.

Hungry Critters

Although I like cardboard boxes and feel they certainly have a place in organizing, I don't like to see them used in the garage. Critters (think rodents and roaches, for starters) feast on cardboard. Why invite them in for a snack? Plastic containers work best here, I think. A word to the wise: some stores sell really large plastic storage tubs. You need to consider what you're going to put in them. Will you be able to move it when it's full?

Whatever you choose to store your possessions in, keep your containers in categories—that is, stored in specific areas of the garage. If you designate an area for seasonal items, for example, be sure that the Fourth of July and Halloween decorations are not mixed. We're doing this to save time in the future.

Perilous Pitfalls

Keep all poisons and toxic chemicals safely out of the reach of young children and animals. A high shelf or a locked cupboard will protect the vulnerable members of your household.

Above all else, don't forget to label the contents. A label maker or labels generated from your computer are best. As I get older, I can't read my own handwriting. Have you found that to be true for yourself? You want everyone to easily identify the contents of a box without having to call you out to the garage for a translation of what's written on the box.

The Sporting Life

If you have kids and teens in your home and you lead an active lifestyle, you are probably overrun by balls, bats, and gloves. Take heart. They now make special holders for all sports equipment. These are not expensive and can be in place in minutes. Some are simple containers that you put together with specific areas for different pieces of equipment. Of course, you can also find more elaborate systems.

The Container Store will tailor its Elfa system to your needs. A garage or closet company can come out and provide a free custom design and cost estimate for the entire garage. You might want to speak with a few companies and compare designs and bids. All custom systems come at a price; you can spend anywhere from $500 to several thousand. It all depends on your items, your intended use and frequency, whether you rent or own your home, and, in the end, the depth of your pocketbook.

Will It Fly?

Remember how I said that we can do things in the garage that we can't do anywhere else in the home for storage? Well, the most unique solution available to us is "flying things." For the latest and the greatest in this arena, begin your quest by either going to your local home store, using Google, and/or calling some hobby shops to see what they have for the items you want to fly.

Bicycles, for example, can be mounted on the wall. If no one is available to help you put the hook or pulley system in place, why not use a bike stand? This way, your bike(s) won't be languishing against your valuable wall space or, worse, scattered on the floor like trash. Bikes aren't the only things you can fly.

> **Perilous Pitfalls**
>
> A dolly is a great tool to have in your garage. If you don't need or want one permanently, see if you can rent or borrow one during the declutter process. If it helps you move several boxes at a clip to the dumpsite, it's worth the effort.

I have a contractor friend who is an avid windsurfer. He uses a simple system of pulleys to keep his equipment aloft. When he's ready to go to the beach, he backs his SUV underneath the equipment and lets the pulleys do the work of gently depositing the equipment into place. You can find bike and sport equipment pulley systems for less than $50. I used Google and found them at several places, including the ever reliable L.L. Bean.

The Hobby Zone

Beyond the basic toolbox lies a world that enables some of us to build all manner of things. Where, however, is one going to use a saw without getting sawdust into everything? The answer, of course, is the humble garage. If the jumble in here has prevented you from setting up a hobby area, now you should see the possibilities.

Baby Steps

When it comes to outfitting a hobby area in the garage, here are the first steps you can take:

1. Declutter the space so you know where your tools, workbench, and other items will go.

2. Decide exactly what type of work you'd like to do here and how extensively you want your hobby area "tricked out," as the kids today like to say. This is the kind of space that can eat up funds, so be sure you are satisfying a long-held desire and not just bankrolling a whim.

3. Confer with a specialist in this field. Start with your local home store and/or a trusted and experienced friend. Consult hobby magazines and stores, and, of course, Google your brains out.

A Kindler, Gentler Hobby

When I think of a hobby area in the garage, I think of my dad with a hammer, nails, and a saw making some bookcases for my room. In today's world, you might want an area where you can have a worktable and shelves above with your scrapbooking supplies.

Some parents also create a zone here where the kids can play with messy things like paints. If they decorate this floor, it isn't as serious as doing the same to the new carpet.

Your hobby zone might be for the creation of a workout area. Your hobby zone could be for something I've never imagined. The bottom line is that you will have reclaimed wasted space and dedicated it to something you enjoy.

The Devil Is in the Details

If you decide you want to make serious year-round use of the garage, you may want to consult with a contractor. Perhaps the walls need to be insulated. Perhaps you need a better light source. Be sure to consult with the pros after you have an idea of the new purpose of the space and how often it will be used. In Los Angeles, for example, when folks turn an area of their garage into a workout space, they need to take into account the blistering heat of the summer months. You need a large fan to cool you off, or just plan on using the space late at night or early in the morning. Consider all the angles.

Beyond the World of Flying Objects

In the garage, you have another advantage: besides flying objects, you can mount them on the wall. In the home, hanging things on the wall is an art. Here it's totally utilitarian, and we can use more of the wall to make life easier. For example, tools with long handles like brooms, shovels, rakes, and mops are great when hung in a simple unit that you can install on the wall of the garage. Now you won't have them falling all over the place, getting dirty, or tripping you up.

You'll also find units that will enable you to keep frequently used smaller tools within easy reach by mounting them on the wall as well.

You can go one step further and find units with wheels that hold the long-handled tools upright. This way you can have them at your disposal as you move about the garage.

Seasonal Fiesta

Some families love to decorate for every holiday, and over the years, their collections grow. Items like these are precious, and eliminating some can be a difficult experience. Take the time to transfer these items to large plastic containers on wheels if they are now in cardboard. Wrap every fragile item in tissue paper. As you go through, if you find that some of the items are worn, torn, frayed, or broken, and well beyond repair, say goodbye to them.

You can divide your decorations into types and put the different categories into the size of container that best suits the number you have. Types for Christmas, for example, might be tree balls, ornaments, and lights. These containers stack easily. You can roll a complete holiday stack into a corner of the garage or loft (see the next section, "Lofty Solutions").

When you want your decorations, they will pull out easily rather than being buried behind a maze of clutter.

> **Timely Tidbits**
> When it comes to holiday decorations like delicate balls for your tree, sometimes it's best to keep the original boxes and place these in your containers.

Lofty Solutions

If you can't afford or don't need a complete garage makeover, you may find the addition of a loft to be a lifesaver. You can store your containers up here and keep the garage floor clear for your car, gardening tools, and perhaps an extra baker's rack as a makeshift pantry for backup items (think paper towels, tissues, toilet paper, cleaners, and so on). Depending on the size of your garage, you may also gain space to create your hobby area.

By the way, be careful if you store items like the family suitcases in the rafters. This area is used by many as a makeshift loft space, but it isn't designed to carry extra weight and can bow over time. Consider putting in a loft or using some of the shelving units I cover next.

Portable Shelves

What do you do with the containers once they are filled? You may have a variety of styles, and not all will be stacked on wheels. Shelves are a lifesaver. I usually go to Bed Bath and Beyond for a baker's rack or I get the same type of product in a store like Home Depot. The latter carries a shelving unit that looks like it goes in a garage. These are usually gray and very utilitarian. The good thing about the baker's rack is that it could live in the house later. Both units are well under $100 and are easy to assemble. When we get your items in the appropriate containers, you can see how many shelving units you need. Our goal is to have a clean, open floor.

If you have a small house and no pantry, a rack right outside the door that leads into the house from the garage is a great location for storing extra toilet paper, paper towels, cleaners, and so on. Cans of food are okay, but I would hesitate to put boxes of cereal or pasta here; once again, these are an invitation to critters to come and dine. Extra water and soda can also be stored here. If Fido's dry kibble is to be kept in the garage, be sure you pour it into an airtight container. And be sure you close it after each use!

It's a Disaster

Gotcha, didn't I? At this point, your garage is probably really taking shape. You may even be wondering why you didn't do this sooner. If you live in an area prone to earthquakes, fires, floods, hurricanes, or any other type of natural disaster, contact the Red Cross and get a list of supplies you need to have on hand. If you invest in camping equipment as part of your disaster preparedness, be sure you place it in the garage so you can easily access it in an emergency. It can serve you only if you can get to it!

Archive Heaven

The garage is the perfect place to put your archived files. It's nice if you can put them into a metal filing cabinet and keep it locked. Once a year, as you bring out the latest material to back up your current income tax return, be sure to toss the year that is now obsolete. Shred everything with an account number or your Social Security number. Don't forget: your actual return is to be kept forever. You may want to keep those in your office.

As much as I like everything labeled, I wouldn't put "Taxes" on the front of the file drawer or on the containers, if you use those instead. Use a code word. If you have repair people coming in and out, or if you frequently leave your garage door open, you don't want to tempt anyone. The label "Taxes" is an invitation to a treasure trove of your identify information.

Perilous Pitfalls

Check with the person who prepares your income tax return to see how many years he or she wants you to keep receipts that represent your tax deductions. This person will have the most up-to-date information. You don't want to be caught without these important documents in the event of an audit.

The Family Car: Vehicle or Storage Vault?

If your car is a disaster, please know that you are in the comfortable majority. An organized car is a rarity. No matter why you drive or how you use your vehicle, we can get it in order. If you are a mom with kids piling in and out, you will need to be vigilant about cleaning out the interior. This can be one of your new habits. Better yet, the kids can have rotating chores, and car maintenance can be on that list.

You know by now that the first step here is to clean out the clutter. Do you have candy wrappers here? Have old food containers been abandoned? Do toys that were once treasured companions now languish on the floor? Let's get it all out into the trash or to its proper home.

Any Gloves in Your Glove Compartment?

Be brave—stick your hand in there and pull out the clutter. It's usually quite amusing what finds its way there. What goes back? I suggest these items:

◆ Frequently referenced maps

◆ A few wet wipes and napkins

◆ An emergency toiletries kit (think small sizes of toothpaste, mouthwash, floss, and perhaps an extra tube of lipstick, if you are a woman)

◆ Some breath mints

◆ Of course, the manual that came with the vehicle

I also keep two quick snacks, like bags of nuts or a health food bar, in case I am caught in heavy traffic.

Rules of the Road for Inside the Vehicle

A wastebasket in the car is a must, as, I think, are tissues and bottles of water. I have scissors and tissues in every room and in my car. Is there any item you like to have in every room? Do you need it in the car?

If you travel with young children, you will have a list specific to their needs. Try to make the items in your vehicle special so they more easily entertain your kids. If you have DVD or CD players, you may want to have a zippered container with your disks tucked neatly inside rather than traveling with the individual jewel cases.

Finally, most school-age kids come into the car at the end of the school day with a plethora of papers. If they get shoved in your face the minute the kids are in the vehicle, keep a special holder in the car for papers. A small (key word) accordion file, for example, could have sections for each child. Tell them to put their information in their section. You can look over everything after dinner or before bed, whichever is your quiet time.

Trunk or Treasure Chest?

To keep the trunk tidy, you can invest in a trunk organizer. There are several varieties on the market. Pick the one that suits what you are going to keep with you. If you are on the road for business, you may want to have a portable file box. You can keep client information here, along with blank forms. This is especially helpful if you are in a paper-heavy profession like real estate.

I must confess that I carry emergency supplies for stray animals in my trunk. It doesn't take up much space to have a small blanket, some canned chicken (don't forget an opener!), and a box of dog biscuits. Because I live in earthquake country, I also have some basic supplies for myself and for my golden retriever. Once again, the trusty local Red Cross will give you an up-to-date list of supplies needed for your car.

Aftermath

The easiest way to keep the garage free of clutter, other than regular maintenance, is to never say the following words: "I don't know what to do with that … just toss it into the garage." If you consider the value of your home, the garage represents valuable square footage. Why not utilize it in a way that serves you, rather than in a way that is constantly creating one big headache?

The Least You Need to Know

♦ A clean, clutter-free garage gives you storage space and a home for your car.

♦ If you have a large garage and/or no need to keep your car inside, you can turn the garage area into a mini bonus room with something like a workout or hobby area, or even a mini pantry.

♦ Space in the garage can be utilized in ways we can't consider in the home. Here things can fly, be hooked up to a pulley system, or cover the entire wall.

Chapter 12

Special Areas in the Home

In This Chapter

♦ Keep your bonus spaces like your mudroom tidy and organized so they all work in concert with your entire home

♦ Reclaim your basement as a true bonus room rather than a storage facility

♦ Don't let your laundry room become cluttered with items that belong in other rooms

♦ Decide whether the attic is a safe place for the items you have placed there

At first blush, you might think this chapter holds no interest for you. After all, how many of us have luxuries like mudrooms and basements? There's always some tip or trick, however, that can be adapted to your situation. As I tell my clients, after all these years, I still read books and magazines on organizing in a quest for some new product I've never seen before or some clever tip I haven't yet used. This old dog loves new tricks!

Having grown up in Brooklyn, New York, these rooms were in just about everyone's home. When I moved west, I was startled to find that things like a hall closet for coats near the front door, any kind of basement or attic, and surely a mudroom were unheard of. Weather, of course, dictates our needs when a home is built. In temperate climates, we don't need a special entryway to help us shake off the snow and the mud. It all makes sense when you think about it, doesn't it? I invite you to kick back, grab your favorite beverage, and spend a few minutes with me in the bonus areas of a home. In case you are inspired in some way, be sure to have your trusty *Declutter Notebook* nearby.

Learn to maximize use of your walk-in pantry and free up other spaces that are now used for food storage. Save steps and save time.

Mudroom: It Isn't Icky Anymore

The mudroom is a great invention, when you think of it. Here we have a place where snow, mud, and rain can fall off our boots, our coats, and our umbrellas without messing up the inside of our house. We can even take a minute to wipe off Fido's paws. In order for the room to work, however, we have to set it up to support us.

Banish the Coat Store Look

During the winter months, we want to be able to shed our boots, coats, and umbrellas here. What resources do you have for that now? In the absence of a small closet here, you can use a portable folding rack like the one I mentioned in the closets chapter. If your mudroom is a tiny affair, you may have room for only a clothes tree or a few sturdy pegs hanging on the wall. In any event, you'll want to have heavy-duty hangers here to hold up under the weight of the average winter coat.

I think you'll find that most coats will be dropped off here to dry and then taken inside to the coat closet. This will prevent the room from getting cluttered with every coat in the home. You may want to leave your knockabout jackets here. I have a golden retriever named Spirit, and I like to easily grab my "dog coat" on the way out for a bathroom break with him.

If the Shoe or Mitten Fits, Know Where to Store 'Em

Very often shoes, especially heavy winter boots, need to drain when you first come into the mudroom. Get some mats for that purpose. In a pinch, good old absorbent newspaper will work. Since a collection of winter shoes and boots scattered across the floor instantly looks like the Clutter Fairy was here, do have a wooden shoe rack to house them when they are dry. Many wooden shoe racks are stackable, so you can provide several shelves for family members if you need them. You may even want to have one set up for adults and one for children.

If the room is large enough, it's nice to have something to sit on so you can lace or zip up your winter boots. Be sly and use a bench that opens up for storage. You can put baskets inside and have gloves, mittens, hats, and scarves waiting. No room to sit? Put up a shelf that can hold baskets with these items inside. Label the shelves in front of each basket so family members know which one to grab.

Has Mary Poppins Been By?

An umbrella stand is perfect here. After they dry, it's nice to have the umbrellas closed and fastened. Several loose umbrellas splayed out in a stand will once again give the look of clutter even if the room is perfectly organized.

Today's Pets Have Stuff of Their Own

If this is Fido's way in and out of the house, during inclement weather you can have two containers: one with dry towels and one for wet ones after you wipe off his paws and his fur. The collapsible mesh holders are nice because you can take the towels directly to the laundry room using the handles. This is a great place to put up a small rack with a few pegs just for Fido's leash, collar, and other items. Some dogs have rain and winter coats of their own. If it's a unit with a shelf, Fido's "poop bags" and brush can be kept here as well.

Are You Ahead of the Game?

As you read my ideas, how many do you have in place for your mudroom? If you need to go shopping, create a Mudroom Shopping List in your *Declutter Notebook*. Take a minute to survey your room in depth. Are some of the coats and jackets tired and not going into the next season? Do you have items here that are best stored elsewhere? It's not uncommon to drop off items here that are meant for the garage. Return everything to its place in your, by now, nicely organized and clutter-free home.

It's nice to have a mirror and perhaps a small table here. You can put down your purse while you take off your coat. You don't want to put grocery bags on a wet floor. Of course, in a small mudroom, your bench might be long enough to accommodate you and your grocery bags. The table would be superfluous. A mirror, however, allows you to check your appearance before you walk out the door. A full-length mirror on the back of the door offers the perfect last-minute view. Finally, if there is space, a garbage can is a nice addition.

> **Timely Tidbits**
>
> Would the kids like something special, like the latest iPod? Put a bank in this room and suggest that everyone drop their loose change here when they enter. The money will go toward the iPod Fund!

Pantry: Any Grub in Here?

A large walk-in pantry is one of the best additions any home can have. In the kitchen chapter, we discuss ways to organize food. You can follow those guidelines here. A large space like this will enable you to bring all of your food items to one area. Perhaps you have stored your beverages, like soda, beer, and bottled water, in the garage in previous homes. Now they can live on the floor of your pantry in designated spots. You may have used several cupboards for food before, and now it can all be in this room. A walk-in pantry provides the kitchen with one-stop shopping on a daily basis.

Are Any Organizing Products Left Over?

I like to use shelf creators in the pantry so I can have several levels of canned goods in one area and still be able to read the labels. This product comes in plastic, metal, or wood so you can coordinate the look in your pantry with that of your kitchen. They also come in various widths to accommodate the various size cans on the market.

I like to use those handy closet shelf dividers here to separate my categories. For example, I like to keep my rice and pasta in one part of a shelf and my soups in another. I label my shelves. These tools all help you because the designated spot for things is clear. You don't have to look on every

Timely Tidbits

Children like to be able to prepare simple meals for themselves. Put items that you don't mind them having access to, like small, single-serving boxes of cereal and juice boxes, on the lower shelf of the pantry so they can learn to be self-sufficient. Keep cookies and candy up high, preferably in containers they can't see through.

shelf for a can of chicken soup, for example. A quick glance at the "soup spot," and you know whether you have any on hand. By the way, anyone who can read can help you unload your grocery bags on shopping day.

Utilize Every Square Inch

On your very top shelves, you can store large but rarely used equipment. You can also keep your paper plates and plastic cutlery here. Move them down when the summer months come if you like to use them for outdoor eating areas. If you want to store items like onions or potatoes in the pantry, put them in pantry baskets or bins. That way, they won't bleed all over a shelf and rob other items of their space.

Safety First—Even in the Smallest Space

Finally, I suggest that you keep all cleaning products and poisons (bug spray, ant powder, and so on) out of the pantry. They may never come in contact with the food, but it's best to keep them apart. What if you pick up a can of bug spray to see if it's still viable and some residue from the last use sticks on your fingers? If you next grab some potatoes or onions for dinner, well, you get the idea. Keep poisons under the sink, and, of course, use a cabinet lock if small children or pets are in the home.

Laundry Room—Fluff and Fold

If you have a laundry room, don't let it become a catchall place. Usually there are some cabinets or at least a shelf above the washer and dryer. Here is where your detergents, spot removers, fabric softener, and other related products should be stored. If you have two shelves, put your backup supplies on the top. Be sure it's reinforced, by the way, because these giant containers of detergent can be quite heavy.

I keep the iron here and any products like spray starch that accompany its use. If you can tuck your ironing board into a wall unit with a door, you have struck laundry room gold. If you don't sew regularly but do basic mending, this room may be the logical spot for your sewing box. Now all of your clean-clothing needs can be taken care of in this one area.

Shed Light on the Subject

This room frequently is a great space for other household items like light bulbs. In a large home, this can be quite a large collection of various sizes. I like to keep them separated on the shelf. If you want, you can use a shelf divider, as we did in your closet. Or you can use one of the rectangular plastic baskets with a handle that we made use of in the bathroom. Be sure to label your shelves and/or your baskets.

Grow Taller in Seconds

If the laundry room is near your bedroom or kitchen (the latter is more common), you can tuck a two-step stool here between the washer and the dryer; it will service the entire floor. If you are short, have a step stool on every floor of the home. You don't want anything to stand in the way of maximizing every square inch of your home. The step stool with no back rail or handle folds to the easiest-to-store size. If you have older or unsteady members of the household, get the step stool with a bar you can hold on to for balance. Whatever choice you make, be safe.

Everyday Details

This is one place where an in-house basic toolbox can be kept with basic tools such as a hammer, a screwdriver, a pliers, some nails, screws, and so on. You may have a few drawers here as well. If you use containers, as we did in the bathrooms and the kitchen (and some drawer liner, of course), you can very nicely divide the small miscellaneous items, like clothespins, buttons, and safety pins, that wind their way to the laundry room. You might even be able to give up the kitchen "junk drawer" and have it here.

If this laundry room is really large and you are blessed with lots of cabinets, these can become storage for extra towels. For instance, this is the perfect spot for beach towels and those you use for Fido. Doesn't every dog have his own stash?

> **Timely Tidbits**
>
> It's wonderful to have fire extinguishers all over the home. The laundry room, garage, and kitchen are especially important places to keep them. Be sure you know how to use one before an emergency strikes.

Look around your laundry room and see if you have other unrelated items here. Now that you have been through your home and organized it, do you see that there is a more appropriate home for these things? Or is it perhaps time to let them go into the circular file? Speaking of trash, be sure you have a wastebasket in this room. If nothing else, you'll fill it with lint from the dryer.

The Attic: What's Lurking Up There?

I have encountered two types of attics. The first I am familiar with is literally a crawl space given the generous name "attic." I would hesitate to use this area because it gets so dirty and usually attracts some kind of creepy crawly. If you absolutely need it, use sturdy plastic containers with airtight locking lids. Label everything and list whatever you put up there so you won't ever say, "I wonder if that missing item is in the attic." Nothing will ever be AWOL again.

Are Aunt Tilly and Uncle Bob Held Hostage Up There?

The other attics I have seen are huge open areas under the roof. They're actual rooms, albeit not ones you would live in. If you have this space, don't make it a repository for everything that doesn't fit in your home. Just because a space exists doesn't mean it has to be filled. And that holds true for every room in your home and every surface in those rooms.

The big-ticket item I see here is furniture. Oddly enough, it's usually furniture you didn't purchase, but inherited. I once had a client who had all of her elderly parents' furniture in her basement. The room was not usable. It looked like a crowded furniture store. Her parents didn't want to sell their stuff or part with it. Her brothers and sisters said they couldn't take it. My client was asked to keep it all. Can you imagine? The hilarious part was that her parents had moved to another state and purchased a condo and all new furniture. They started fresh and left her with their unmade decisions. See how insidious this can be?

Timely Tidbits

Don't use a crawl space attic to store your valuables. This is one of the first places a thief looks because it's one of the most common areas people use.

If you are holding furniture for others, free yourself. All this stuff is quite literally sitting on your head if it's in your attic. It needs to be sent into the world to its rightful owner—even if that new owner is an antique dealer, eBay, or something like Craig's List.

When You Need the Space for Storage

What if the space in your attic needs to be used? After all, even if you don't have a garage or basement, you surely have holiday decorations and assorted miscellaneous items that don't fit into other areas in your home. By all means, use your attic. Be sure you have followed the basic guidelines from all the previous chapters: eliminate what you don't need or no longer use; place the items that are to stay into categories. This helps you determine what organizing solutions will best serve you.

Finally, label everything and be sure it's placed in the attic so that your categories remain together. You don't want a stray box of photos to be hidden under your holiday ornaments. Every type of item you could have up here has been dealt with in detail in one of the previous chapters. Check out the declutter instructions and organizing details presented. In no time, you'll create an attic that's clutter-free, tidy, and well organized.

Whew! It Sure Is Hot Up Here

Storing things in the attic always makes me nervous because the temperature may fluctuate. If you place precious photos here, for example, the summer heat may do irreparable harm to them. Check out the photo storage ideas presented in Chapter 6. If you don't have a family room, you can place your photo collection elsewhere but still use those guidelines to get it under control.

I've Got the Creepy Crawlies

As I mention in Chapter 11, critters like roaches, spiders, and rodents love to feast on cardboard. Don't provide them with a tempting repast. Store your treasures in high-quality plastic containers. And don't forget to label the contents. You may even want to number the boxes and create a reference list on your computer. The next time you wonder if something is up in the attic, all you have to do is check your computer file.

 Timely Tidbits

Create reference lists (for example, what's in your file drawers and what's stored in the attic or garage). Keep a hard copy in a reference notebook. The master file will be in your computer, ready to be updated as you add and delete items. This allows your fingers to literally do the walking when you wonder where you put something you need.

The Basement: Who's Down There?

If you've got a basement, why not utilize the space? If you answer "yes" to any of the following, the basement may be your answer.

- ◆ Would you have more house guests if you had a place for them to sleep?
- ◆ Would you like to work out at home instead of the gym?

◆ Do you think your teenagers need a place to hang out with their friends while still under your watchful eye?

◆ Have the kids left home and left you with the desire to have a hangout for that weekly poker game you gave up 18 years ago?

◆ Would you like to get a pool table and have a total game room?

◆ Is your home-based business successful and in need of a bigger space? Would you like to *start* a home-based business, perhaps one that requires you to store products?

I could go on, but you get the picture. You can convert the basement into the space you have been dreaming about. Don't let this room go to waste as a storage site for all the furniture and boxes you don't really need, especially if these things belong to other family members. If you have kept your home pristine by shuttling all your unmade decisions downstairs, you have unwittingly turned this valuable real estate into Clutter Central.

If you do have some things you feel you must hold on to, see if you can artfully move everything to one side of the room and utilize the rest as a gym, office, or hangout. Perhaps you can place a beautiful screen in front of your treasures so that they have their own area—one that you needn't look at every time you enter. Of course, you'll want to organize these items, not just shove them into that corner.

Sensational Solutions

Here are some questions that will serve as a guideline for you. The other chapters offer organizing solutions for the spaces I have mentioned. Let's move out the debris.

Do you have inherited furniture? Can it be used in your home? Would it be more useful to you if you painted it or refinished it? If you have no realistic intention of using it—say, it just isn't your style—can you offer it to another relative who might appreciate it? Or can you sell it and raise the funds needed to really transform this space into something you will enjoy?

In the absence of a garage or adequate closet space, have you made this room the dumpsite for things like off-season clothes and holiday decorations? Or is it memorabilia and photo-dump central?

Clean out these stashes to whittle your collection down to what you realistically know you will use. Be sure you have everything in attractive containers that are labeled. The storage ideas I cover in the family room chapter for memorabilia and photos could be used here. In addition, you can find portable clothes racks with canvas covers. You can put off-season clothing here, all zipped into an attractive and protected storage unit.

If you need smaller containers, use the ones with wheels. You can have your categories stacked and accessible and oh-so-easy to hide behind a screen.

In the garage, I suggested you use baker's racks. If you have only a few boxes, you can put a rack here and use it to stack your categories. When you assemble the rack, you can adjust the shelves to fit your containers.

If you use throw rugs artfully to mark off areas in the room, people's eyes won't be drawn as easily to your storage. And if they are, they will be impressed with the well-organized presentation. Instead of judging you, they will be inspired to do something like this with their own hidden stashes of stuff.

The Least You Need to Know

- Bonus rooms are a gift to any homeowner. They shouldn't be clogged with storage.

- If you are a homeowner, utilizing every area of your house to the max will help attract buyers when the time comes. Everyone immediately sees the full potential of the home if it's decluttered and organized.

- After reading this book, you will have a wealth of tips and tricks. Think globally and apply your decluttering and organizing skills to all areas of your home.

Appendix A

Further Reading

Psychological/Emotional Issues Books

Beattie, Melody. *Codependent No More: How to Stop Controlling Others and Start Caring for Yourself.* Hazelden, 1986.

Bradshaw, John. *Homecoming: Reclaiming and Championing Your Inner Child.* Bantam Doubleday Dell, 1992.

Organizing Books

Leeds, Regina. *Creating a Place Without Losing Your Space: A Couple's Guide to Blending Homes, Lives, and Clutter.* Alpha Books, 2003.

———. *The Zen of Organizing: Creating Order and Peace in Your Home, Career, and Life.* Alpha Books, 2002.

Feng Shui Books

Carter, Karen Rauch. *Move Your Stuff, Change Your Life: How to Use Feng Shui to Get Love, Money, Respect, and Happiness.* Fireside, 1960.

Kingston, Karen. *Creating Sacred Space with Feng Shui: Learn the Art of Space Clearing and Bring New Energy into Your Life.* Broadway, 1997.

Rossbach, Sarah. *Feng Shui: The Chinese Art of Placement.* Penguin/ Arkana, 1991.

Resources

Organizations

Clutterers Anonymous
www.clutterersanonymous.net

Messies Anonymous
www.messies.com
786-243-2793

Closet Systems

Closets by Design
www.closetsbydesign.com
1-800-293-3744

Organizing Products

Bed Bath & Beyond
www.bedbathandbeyond.com
1-800-462-3966

The Container Store
www.thecontainerstore.com
1-800-733-3532

Hold Everything
www.holdeverything.com
1-800-421-2264

Ikea
www.ikea.com
1-800-434-4532

Lowe's
www.lowes.com
1-800-445-6973

Websites

Exposures
www.exposuresonline.com
1-800-222-4947

Lillian Vernon
www.lillianvernon.com

Reliable Home Office
www.reliablehomeoffice.com
1-800-869-6000

Office Products

Levenger's
www.levenger.com
1-800-667-8034

Office Max
www.officemax.com
1-800-788-8080

Staples
www.staples.com
1-800-STAPLES (1-800-782-7537)

Professional Organizers

National Association of Professional Organizers
www.NAPO.net
1-847-375-4746

Regina Leeds
www.reginaleeds.com
zenorg1@aol.com
818-506-7167

Junk Mail Elimination

Junk Mail Elimination
Mail Preference Service
Direct Marketing Association
P.O. Box 9008
Farmingdale, NY 11735

Miscellaneous

AuctionDrop and **iSold It**
www.auctiondrop.com and
www.i-soldit.com
(They sell on eBay for you.)

Craig's List
www.craigslist.org

eBay
www.ebay.com

Ready, Set, Relax!
www.readysetrelax.org

Real Simple **Magazine**
www.realsimple.com

Index

P–Q